'WHAT WAS FROM THE
BEGINNING'

'WHAT WAS FROM THE BEGINNING'

THE EMERGENCE OF ORTHODOXY IN EARLY CHRISTIANITY

PROSPER GRECH, OSA

GRACEWING

First published in England in 2016
by
Gracewing
2 Southern Avenue
Leominster
Herefordshire HR6 0QF
United Kingdom
www.gracewing.co.uk

ISBN 978 085244 905 9

Typeset by Gracewing

Cover design by Bernardita Peña Hurtado

CONTENTS

PREFACE

CHRISTIANITY IS ONE of the world's great religions. Each religion has striven to maintain its own identity down the ages and seeks to present itself today in the right perspective. Today's Christianity is a conglomeration of Churches and confessions each of which claims to profess the genuine faith in Jesus Christ. Current ecumenical discussions seek to separate the wheat from the chaff and to help all these trends to converge towards an understanding of what really constitutes the core of Christian doctrine. It is not possible to argue about present differences without referring to our beginnings. Such an undertaking is not rendered easier by injecting contemporary ideas into the past. The main question is: how did the Church in the first centuries of her existence resolve her theological and structural problems to reach catholicity through doctrinal, social, political and disciplinary challenges up to the point when she called herself the Catholic Church? This essay is a modest contribution to the ongoing debate about the rise of orthodoxy in early Christianity and the present ecumenical movement. It should be obvious that the subject matter indicated by the title of each chapter cannot be addressed fully. It is addressed with reference to the main thesis of this book. I have tried to keep a neutral attitude insofar as this is possible for an author who belongs to a confession. If I have not succeeded entirely, I entreat the reader to use his or her sense of humour.

I express my gratitude to Professor Hubertus Drobner and Dr Matthew Fforde for reading through the manuscript and offering constructive historical, theological and stylistic suggestions. I owe my thanks to Chabi Kolawole for his invaluable help with the bibliography and notes.

INTRODUCTION

We declare to you what was from the beginning,
what we have heard, what we have seen with
our eyes, what we have looked at and touched
with our hands, concerning the word of life.

1Jn 1:1

THE OPENING OF John's First Epistle explains the title of this book whose aim is to collect and evaluate the criteria the Fathers of the early Church used to distinguish correct from false doctrines in the first four centuries.

The present debate on the relationship between ancient 'Christianities' began with the publication in 1934 of Walter Bauer's book *Rechtgläubigkeit und Ketzerei im ältesten Christentum*. In this work, he argued that so-called heresy preceded orthodoxy in most of the Churches of very early Christianity.[1] This certainly caused a stir among patristic scholars and the book was criticised from many points of view. In spite of all objections, it opened a new chapter in the study of the first Christian centuries. Which strand of Christianity should be considered 'orthodox' and which 'heretical'? Who decides? The title of Bart Ehrman's book, *Lost Christianities: the Battles for Scripture and Faiths we Never Knew*, poses the problem very well.[2]

In the second century, Pauline, Johannine, Jewish-Christian and Gnostic communities coexisted, often in conflict with each other. Were they all on a par as if in a kind of religious supermarket? If not, which were the actual criteria that led to some groups and doctrines to be

discarded in favour of what came to be called Catholic or
mainstream Christianity? The problem has no easy solution as many arguments can lead to a vicious circle. For
example, one can argue that 'Christian' is everything that
agrees with the New Testament, but others would say that
the New Testament canon was actually defined by some
Christians to exclude others, with the setting aside of many
other writings that claimed to be apostolic.[3]

It may not be totally untrue to say that this historical
relativism reflects today's relativistic mentality, but this is
not an excuse to take the matter lightly. The question is:
what method must be used to define what is Christian and
what is not, and to determine whether there was a hard
doctrinal core in the earliest Jesus groups which served as
a standard criterion. We shall begin by outlining Bauer's
thesis and then seek the best approach to achieving a
reasonable solution.

Bauer begins by examining the Churches of Edessa and
Egypt. In the former, it was only in the fourth century that
orthodoxy was imposed by Rabhula and Kune on the
majority of Bardesanites, Marcionites and Manichees. The
Abgar legend was invented to justify this imposition. In
Egypt, too, we find no orthodox document prior to
Clement of Alexandria. Like Kune in Edessa, it was Bishop
Demetrius who enforced 'right doctrine' upon the Gnostic
majority. The Mark legend, like the Abgar legend in
Edessa, lent force to this victory.

In Asia Minor, Ignatius and Polycarp made use of
monarchical episcopacy to impose mastery over a majority
of Gnostics. Asian Gnosticism was born within Paulinism.
After 70 CE many Jewish Christians fled to Asia and allied
themselves with the Pauline Churches against the Gnostics
who gradually abandoned the assemblies. The four clauses
in Acts 15 were enforced and gentile Christians were freed

from the ceremonial institutions of the Torah. However, in Asia orthodoxy only reached as far as Hierapolis in the second century and was in a minority in Antioch. The letters in Rev 2–3 hinted at the fact that of the seven Churches only four were approved—the rest being seen as heading towards heresy. Later there was a wide circulation of books by the Montanists and Montanism itself became very popular. The Church's Bible was the Old Testament which could not be used against the Marcionites and Gnostics who did not acknowledge its authority. Matthew and Mark were received immediately, Luke and John later: the former because it was favoured by Marcion; the latter because it was suspected of Gnostic leanings.

As to Rome, 1 Clement combats Gnosticism in Corinth, and this city, bribed by Roman 'charities', became the bridge over which the authority of Peter and Paul, and that of the Bishop of Rome, invaded Asia and Syria. Paul, too, was not popular in the second century owing to his reception by Marcion, thanks to whom his letters were preserved and helped to exclude Jewish Christians. The Pastoral Letters were composed to save the figure of Paul for the Church. Paul had no regard for the earthly Jesus and his was only a theological outline of Christ. It was through the Synoptics that the historical figure of Jesus was kept alive.

The Roman mind was logical and could not understand Eastern syncretistic thought. Furthermore, the Roman Church was organised whereas the Gnostics were spread here and there. This was the reason for its increasing authority. Ultimately, however, it was Constantine and the Roman State that established this Church, in which, however, the 'orthodox' remained a minority.

Many of Bauer's sweeping statements could only provoke an academic earthquake and many objections were raised to Bauer's thesis, not least that the book contained various historical errors. Indeed, the English translation *Orthodoxy and Heresy in Early Christianity* of 1971 included an appendix by Georg Strecker with various comments on the book and its reception.[4]

It should be borne in mind that in 1934 the idea that there was a pre-Christian Gnosticism was still prevalent.[5] It is common knowledge today that we cannot speak strictly of Gnosticism existing before the beginning of the second century. The Messina definition and the so-called Yale School later altered these propositions. Yet Bauer set the ball rolling and the contention that there were various Christianities in the first centuries gained ground. Today, the question of how and when the 'orthodoxy' of the mainstream Church prevailed is still open to further study.

The question is how the problem should be approached. What distinguishes a Christian from a non-Christian or semi-Christian religion? The very word 'religion', which presupposes some sort of doctrine, ethics and worship, is ambiguous because it would not apply to some Gnostic communities who were nearer to what we call today 'theosophies'. Again, one can give an *a priori* definition of Christianity—broadening or narrowing it to suit precon- ceived conclusions.

For example, we can apply the adjective 'Christian' to a faith which has a connection with the historical figure of Jesus of Nazareth, or that accepts Jesus as the Christ. But what if Jesus' body was not real (Docetism), or if Christ and Jesus were two separate entities? Again, can we dissociate Christianity from the Old Testament and Judaism, or the Christian God from the God of the Jews? Is there a black- and-white distinction between a Christian and a non- Christian, or can many shades of grey lie in between, in the sense of degrees of personal adherence and doctrine?[6]

It seems to me that the least objectionable way to provide some answers to these questions is to examine the documents of the first century, namely those produced by people who were nearer in time to Jesus and his movement. This, of course, would include the writings of the New Testament, not because they were subsequently canonised but because they are more able—from a chronological perspective—to inform us about the self-definition of those who were first known as 'Nazarenes' or 'Christians' in the first-century. Other Apostolic Fathers, like the Didache, 1Clement, Hermas and Barnabas can also be invoked as belonging to earliest Christianity.

What questions must we pose to these witnesses of the early Church? First of all, was there a central confession that held the Churches together? How did they distinguish between erroneous and acceptable confessions? Were the different theological strands—Pauline, Jewish Christian and Johannine—mutually complementary or were they in conflict with one another? Did they dovetail with Judaism or was there a clean break from it?[7] Was the Old Testament still held to be valid? How did outsiders view these communities? And, last but not least, can we deduce from the answers to these questions some sort of criterion by which to distinguish orthodox thought from the erroneous interpretations of later centuries?

In chapter one, I offer some inevitably debatable conclusions which I then develop in subsequent chapters.

Notes

1. English translation: W. Bauer, *Orthodoxy and Heresy in Earliest Christianity* (London, 1972). This edition contains an appendix with some comments on Bauer's thesis by various authors.
2. B. Ehrman, *Lost Christianities: the Battles for Scripture and Faiths we Never Knew* (Oxford, 2003). For a moderate position cf. J.

O'Grady, *Early Christian Heresies* (New York, 1985). More radical are M. Edwards, *Catholicity and Heresy in the Early Church* (Farnham, 2009) and G. Lüdemann, *Ketzer: Die andere Seite des frühen Christentums* (Stuttgart, 1996).

3. It should be remembered that there was no definition of a canon in the early Church. We find lists in Eusebius for example, and a semi-official list in a council in Carthage in 393 that was accepted throughout the Middle Ages. The Catholic Roman Church only defined its canon at the Council of Trent.

4. Apart from some sweeping statements, Bauer was mainly criticised for his frequent practice of arguing from silence.

5. Complications arose because the Germans used 'Gnosis' and 'Gnostizismus' in more or less the same sense. After the Messina Conference in 1951 the term Gnosticism was reserved for the second and third century Gnostic systems, while gnosis indicated earlier Hellenistic speculation on the liberating quality of knowledge.

6. Ehrman has a whole chapter on this subject: See Ehrman, *Lost Christianities*, pp. 91–116.

7. The question about the definite break of Christianity from Judaism is still hotly debated: see F. Blanchetière, *Enquete sur les raciness juives du movement chrétien* (Paris, 2001); S. C. Mimouni, *Les chrétiens d'origine juive dans l'antiquité* (Paris, 2004).

1 THE EARLIEST PROCLAMATION

ROCLAMATION OR KERYGMA, as distinct from *didaché*, theology and *parenesis*, is the straightforward announcement of an axiom about God or Christ which should be accepted on the authority of an apostle. *Didache* is further instruction on, and deepening of, the proclamation; theology is the rational expansion of both, while parenesis is the exhortation to follow the moral rules that arise from faith. For example, in 1Cor 15 Paul announces the reality of bodily resurrection based on the fact of the resurrection of Jesus. This is followed by an explanation of how the resurrection of the body can be understood. Col 3 draws the moral consequences of baptismal resurrection foreshadowing the resurrection of the body. In John 11:23–27 we find a profession of faith in the resurrection.

Was there a uniform proclamation in apostolic times? C.H. Dodd reconstructed the kerygma from the speeches in Acts and passages from the Pauline writings.[1] Many scholars accepted his suggestion, as indeed I did fifty years ago. Further studies on this question, however, especially those by Käsemann,[2] convinced me that there was a plurality of ways of proclaiming the Kingdom: Acts portrays the Jerusalem tradition; the Pauline letters Paul's; and the Johannine literature has its own kerygma. In the Gospels, Matthew writes for a Jewish Christian community and Mark is said to have reflected Peter's preaching. That these various sources contain different theologies and ways of proclamation is clear, but can we speak of a common

backbone of both proclamation and confessions of faith that
define a core of doctrine shared by all of Jesus' followers?

Paul's evangelisation of Jews and God-fearing gentiles
in Corinth was centred on the view that 'Christ died for
our sins in accordance with the Scriptures, and that he
was buried, and that he was raised on the third day in
accordance with the Scriptures, and that he appeared to
Cephas, then to the twelve' (1Cor 15:3–6). He reminds the
gentiles in Thessalonica 'how you turned to God from
idols, to serve a living and true God, and to wait for his
Son from heaven, whom he raised from the dead—Jesus,
who rescues us from the wrath that is coming' (1Thess
1:9–10). There had been no need to tell the Corinthians
that there was one true and living God, but in Thessalonica
conversion to the one God was a necessity. This recalls
the story in Acts 14:8–18 of how Paul and Barnabas
announced monotheism to simple people in Lystra, and
Luke's Demosthenic version of Paul's words on the Are-
opagus in Athens (Acts 17:22–31).

Again in Rom 1:3–4 Paul announces the event pre-
dicted by the prophets: 'the gospel concerning his Son,
who was descended from David according to the flesh and
was declared to be Son of God with power according to
the spirit of holiness by the resurrection form the dead,
Jesus Christ our Lord'. In Rom 16:25–27 the apostle adds
the revelation of the mystery of the inclusion of the
gentiles in salvation through their obedience of faith.

In the Acts of the Apostles, Luke seeks to reconstruct
Peter's kerygma in Jerusalem and Paul's kerygma in Antioch
from traditional patterns of preaching, including proof passages from the Old Testament (2:14–36; 3:12–26; 13:16–41).

Do we find any kerygmayic formulas in John?[3] It is highly
probable that Jesus' words to Nicodemus in John 2:16–19,
whether addressed to him or not, summarise the whole

gospel of the Beloved Disciple: 'For God so loved the world that he gave his only Son, so that everyone who believes in him may not perish but may have eternal life. Indeed, God did not send the Son to condemn the world, but in order that the world might be saved through him. Those who believe in him are not condemned; but those who do not believe are condemned already, because they have not believed in the only Son of God. And this is the judgment, that the light has come into the world, and people loved darkness rather than light because their deeds were evil'. The message is repeated in 1John 4:9–10. We find the Pauline version of the Father's undeserved love in Rom 5:5–11, with the added emphasis on Christ's death for us.

It is evident that the event of Christ is approached from various angles by Luke, Paul and John. Is there a common denominator? Eugene E. Lemcio addresses this problem in his book *The Past of Jesus in the Gospels.*[4] He examines the four gospels, Acts, Rom, 2Cor, Gal, Eph, Phil, Col, 1Thess, 1 and 2 Tim, Tit, Heb, 1Pet, 1John and Rev. The general conclusion, supported by texts outside the NT (1Clem, Polycarp, Diognetus, Justin, Acts of Paul and Thecla), is that all these documents have six points in common: 1 God, 2 who sent/raised, 3 Jesus, 4 response of reception: repentance and 5 faith in God that 6 brings variously described benefits. Lemcio says that the convergence is more theocentric than Christocentric.

Lemcio, however, was comparing pre-Easter and post-Easter announcements and responses. In n. 4 he lists 'faith'. It is precisely this response of faith that we must now examine more deeply. There are many confessions of faith in almost all the New Testament documents.[5] They mirror the cognate announcements of the gospel in the early communities: 'If you confess with your lips that Jesus is Lord and believe in your heart that God raised him from the dead, you will be saved. For one believes with the heart and so is justified, and one confesses with the mouth and so is saved' (Rom 10: 9). These homologies can be simple acclamations: 'You are the Son of God', 'My Lord and my God'; verbal or nominal sentences, i.e. when the predicate is a verb or a noun; or simple or multiple ones, like the one just quoted. They are mainly Christological. Jesus is confessed as the Christ among the Jews and among the gentiles as Lord; he is the Son of God, the Saviour of the world, he died for our sins, and he rose (was raised) again from the dead.

The *Sitz im Leben* of these confessions was mainly in the context of charismatic prayer: 'No one can say "Jesus is Lord" except by the Holy Spirit' (1Cor 12:3). In the Gospel of John each of Jesus' miracles is followed by an 'I am' saying and by a confession. Furthermore, confessions inspired by the Holy Spirit were made before tribunals: 'When they hand you over, do not worry how you are to speak or what to say; for what you are to say will be given to you at that time; for it is not you who speak, but the Spirit of your Father speaking through you' (Mt 10:19). It was the Spirit of the Father who inspired Peter's confession at Caesarea (Mt 16:16). Stephen's confession in Acts 7:56 is the first example of a confession before a tribunal.

When deviations from what had been preached occurred, homologies confessed the right doctrine. For example against Docetic tendencies: 'By this you know the Spirit of God: every spirit that confesses that Jesus Christ has come in the flesh is of God, and every spirit that does not confess Jesus is not from God' (1Jn 4:2; and cf. 5:6–12). We shall see later that baptismal interrogations formed the backbone of Christian self-identity. Paul's answer to the jailer's question in Acts 16:28–32 may have been their forerunner.

These confessions later coalesced to form the *regula fidei*, from which the official creeds were born.

Confessions were also found in the so-called New Testament hymns, as in John 1:1–18; Phil 2:2–15; Col 1:15–20; 1Tim 3:16; and 1Pt 2:21–25. Consequently, the *lex orandi* became the *lex credendi*. Moreover, as some of these 'hymns' predated their written form and reveal a high Christological confession, we can conclude that faith in Christ's divinity arose quite early, at least in Pauline and Johannine communities. This would have meant that certain Jewish Christian groups who did not rise above the confession of Jesus's status as the Messiah were left behind. They were later absorbed into Ebionite communities.[6] The title 'Son of God' could be interpreted in many ways as it developed towards its ontological stability.

We now come to our main point. From what we have said, it is clear that in the early Church there were various ways of announcing God's salvation through Christ, and various ways of receiving it. The assimilation of the evolution of confessions of faith was not homogeneous among all the believing communities. However, can we make a distinction between diversity and error? Are the 'Christianities' we find in the New Testament documents mutually exclusive or are they so complementary that they were able to be included later in one canon illustrative of the Rule of Faith? And, if we do speak of possible erroneous doctrines in the first century, what were the criteria for discernment between acceptable pronouncements and error? To answer this question, we must examine some individual texts that enlighten us as regards the arguments used by the various authors to reject certain doctrines.

Before we do so, however, it is useful to recall certain categories of Jews who were frowned upon in the first century.[7] A *meshummad* was a person who publicly disregarded observance of the Torah, whether from contempt or negligence. In Palestine a *min* was a person who belonged to some fringe or other of Judaism but it could also denote in Babylon a gentile, who was usually called a *goy*. This category included the *nosrim*, i.e., the Nazarenes or Christians. *Minim* fell under the curse of the twelfth 'blessing' in the *shimoneh 'eshreh* which was recited three times a day. An *apiqoros* (from 'epicurean') was sceptical about God's intervention in human affairs. Perhaps even the Sadducees belonged to this category. Judaism defined itself in relation to the Covenant and observance of the Torah; it was an orthopraxis unlike the orthodoxy of the Christians, whose self-definition was centred on belief in Jesus the Messiah. Hence, the term that later prevailed in the Church was *hairesis*, which in itself means a faction, but it acquired the technical meaning of heresy after the fourth century.

In essence, a teaching is false if it swerves away from that of 'the Lord'. He is the ultimate authority. Paul appeals to the Lord in 1Cor 7:10–25 when speaking about marriage and celibacy and again in 1Cor 11 when referring to the Eucharist. The fact that all four Gospels report the sayings of Jesus even when it is their own theological development that is attributed to the Lord means that they were aware of a development of Jesus's doctrine in the sense of John 16:5–15—a development guided by the Holy Spirit.

We find the earliest examples of this in the First Letter to the Corinthians. In 1:10–16 Paul rebukes the community which is split into factions or parties that side with Paul, Cephas or Apollo. He finds this intolerable as the community belongs to Christ, not to any individual apostle. Similar cases later on are called schisms: they sin against the *koinonia* of charity rather than against right doctrine.

In 1Cor 5:1–5 we find the first case of a formal excommunication in the Church. A member of the Corinthian community was having an affair with his stepmother. In rabbinic terms, he was a *meshummad*. Paul uses the strongest possible language to condemn this scandal and, imagining himself present among the congregation, he orders: 'You are to hand over this man to Satan for the destruction of the flesh, so that his spirit may be saved in the day of the Lord'. The man is excluded from the *koinonia* of the community, and, like Judas, goes out into the night. The excommunication is only medicinal however; its purpose is the sinner's conversion.

In chapter 15 the apostle corrects a very serious error in the Corinthians' interpretation of the resurrection of the body. Greek anthropology envisaged the soul as being imprisoned in the body; it is freed when the body dies. Why, therefore, enslave the soul to it once more? Paul's Jewish anthropological viewpoint was that the human being was an animated body; without the body the person is incomplete, and loses their full identity. Paul does not counter this idea by means of philosophical arguments; he appeals to the kerygma 'that was from the beginning' and points to the resurrection of Christ as a fact which cannot be denied because of its numerous witnesses, himself included. The old adage says contra factum non datur argumentum: there is no argument against actual fact. If, therefore, Christ did rise from the dead the resurrection of the body is factually possible. The Christian rises not only as Jesus rose, but because Jesus rose. As the Letter to the Corinthians makes clear in chapter 12, we form one body with Christ and share the same destiny. Moreover, if Christ did not rise from the dead this would cut the ground from under the feet of our whole faith; existence loses its whole purpose: an *argumentum ex absurdo*.

The Letter to the Galatians presents us with a good example of discernment. Jewish Christians from Jerusalem had arrived among the Galatians and almost convinced

them that Paul's preaching about justification by faith was
false. They should receive circumcision and observe the
Law if they meant to become fully Christian. This touched
Paul's most sensitive nerve and his reaction is the most
vigorous we find in all his writings. He begins by asserting
that his apostleship was given to him directly by Christ
(1:1). The gospel he had preached to them did not have
human origins—it had been revealed to him directly by
Jesus Christ (1:11–12). Therefore: 'Even if we or an angel
from heaven should proclaim to you a gospel contrary to
what we proclaimed to you, let that one be accursed!' (1:9).
Apart from this claim, what reasons does he adduce in
support of his thesis? First of all, he tells the Galatians that
Peter, James and John were in agreement with him at the
'council' in Jerusalem (1:18–24; 2:6–10). This is the first
appeal to a 'council' and to the authority of the main
apostles to be found in the history of theology. He then
supports his claim with an appeal to Scripture (1:16=Ps
243:2). There is yet another argument *ex absurdo* (2: 21):
if justification is derived through the works of the Law
then Christ died in vain. His main argument, however, is
that this community had received the gift of the Spirit
which was manifest in their charisms (3:2–5): *ubi Spiritus
ibi salus*; the presence of the Spirit is the main sign of
God's approval. It was these adversaries, not Paul, who did
not understand the Christian message.

Paul's adversaries persecuted him even after his death
and would have brought about a *damnatio memoriae* had
not Luke written the Acts of the Apostles, which, in
substance, are the acts of Peter and Paul.[8] The narrative
first of all prepares the Church for a long history. It stresses
the point that it was not Paul, but Peter, by means of a
special revelation, who had admitted the gentiles without
requiring circumcision. The gift of the Spirit before

baptism had indicated the way Peter should act (ch. 10). In chapter 15 he describes what happened at the apostles' meeting in Jerusalem about which we have already been informed by Paul in Gal 2:6–10. The 'columns of the church', Peter, James and John, had given a free hand to Paul to preach to the gentiles without requiring circumcision and observance of the Torah. Everywhere the apostle preached his gospel the Spirit had confirmed his message with signs and special gifts until he reached Rome. Acts merits the title of Paul's Apologia.

The circulation of the four Gospels after Paul's death represented the four aspects of what came to be called 'mainstream Christianity'. Matthew was the Gospel of moderate Jewish Christians; Mark contained Peter's tradition; Luke, Paul's; and John was the Gospel of the Johannine communities in Asia. The Letter to the Ephesians, therefore, can now speak of 'the Church', in its catholic aspect; the bride of Christ as Israel was the Bride of Yahweh. Its exhortation is to maintain 'the unity of the Spirit in the bond of peace. There is one body and one Spirit, just as you were called to the one hope of your calling, one Lord, one faith, one baptism, one God and Father of all, who is above all, and through all and in all' (Eph 4:3–6). Jewish Christians open to the admission of the gentiles continued to exist and they had Matthew as their gospel. The Gospels of the Hebrews and of the Nazarenes, about which we know so little, also belonged to Jewish-Christian groups. As has already been observed, the hard-core anti-Pauline groups gradually fell out or were absorbed into the Ebionite faction.

The post-Pauline and the Pastoral Letters were instrumental in establishing Paul's communities in Asia Minor. Difficulties were bound to arise, however. In Paul's time there was some Jewish speculation about angels and the

figure of Melchizedek, as is obvious in 11Q Melchisedek.
Official Judaism condemned the adoration of angels, but
in this document it seems that Melchizedek was regarded
by some as an angelic figure with redemptive and escha-
tological connotations. Some Jewish converts to Christianity may have brought with them these speculations and
applied them to a developing Christology. In Phrygia and
in the Lykos valley they were possibly mixed with local
cults and mystery religions by fringes of Judaism to
interpret Christ as an angelic being (cf. also *The Ascension
of Isaiah)*. Were the Christians of Colossae infected by
these speculations? This is not impossible, given some
obscure terms in Col 2:8–18, and this accounts for the
emphasis in the hymn in 1:15–20 on the fact that Christ
is the *creator* of all angelic beings, dominions and princi-
palities. The suspicion is stronger in the Epistle to the
Hebrews which dedicates its first two chapters to clarifying
the distinction between Christ, the Son of God, and the
angels. It appeals to 'what we have heard' (2:1) and to
numerous citations from Scripture in chapter 1. It is not
impossible that these eclectic ideas may have been the
precursors of full-blown Gnosticism in the second century. Scripture, the *lex orandi* and the early preaching are
brought in to correct this error.

The Epistle to the Hebrews is also useful in giving us
an insight into the elementary *didaché* in the communities
to which it is addressed: the renunciation of dead works
(perhaps including the 'Two Ways'), faith in God, teaching
on baptisms, the laying on of hands, the resurrection of
the dead, and eternal judgment (6:1–2).

Many scholars consider 2Thess as pseudographical and
see it as written later, on the model of 1Thess. In this letter
we find an emphasis on tradition as memory. Speaking of
the Antichrist 'Paul' says: 'Do you not remember that I

told you these things when I was still with you?' (2:5). In 2:2 he warns the Thessalonians not to be deceived by prophecy, word or letters purporting to be his. They should 'Stand firm and hold fast to the traditions that you were taught by us either by word of mouth or by letter' (2:15). Apostolic tradition is thus authenticated as authoritative. The mention of a letter claiming to be by Paul is of great interest if 2Thess was itself not Paul's but written later in his name. That would mean that a 'false' letter was denouncing another false letter. What distinguished them? The author of 2Thess would have claimed that he represented the genuine Pauline tradition whereas the other letter was a fake. The fact that 2Thess, and not the other, was later accepted as canonical, means that the mainstream Church found its faith mirrored in this epistle.

Hitherto we have spoken of errors, not of heresy. Towards the end of the first century, or the beginning of the second, however, the Pastoral Letters reveal that certain people or groups held false ideas that approach heresy, not only in the sense of factions but also of erroneous doctrines held and disseminated with a certain level of obstinacy.

1Tim, 2Tim and Tit form a group of letters written in the name of Paul by one of his 'school' to assert their doctrine with apostolic authority and apply Paul's tenets to their historical situations. It is not impossible, as Hanson suggested, that that may have included, and worked over, some genuinely Pauline papers that were still in circulation.[9]

It is not easy to identify the group against whom these letters are directed; nor do we know whether they were one group or many. We can only list some of their characteristics as found in the Pastorals. They seem to have been Jewish converts who cultivated 'myths' and

human commandments (Tit 1:10–16); they spoke of the
Law (1Tim 1:3–11); they appealed to a 'false gnosis' (1Tim
6:20s); they prohibited marriage and certain foods (1Tim
4:1–16); and loved 'interminable genealogies' (Tit 3:9–11).
Two names are mentioned, Hymenaeus and Alexander
(1Tim 1:18–20), who were excommunicated by 'Paul', as
well as Hymenaeus and Philetus who asserted that the
resurrection of the dead had already taken place (2Tim
2:18). All these *hairetikoi andres* should be warned again
and again, but if they do not listen they should be cast out
because they bring about disunity (Tit 3:19).

If all these characteristics belonged to one group of
people, they would have been some heterodox Jews who
dabbled in Hellenistic speculations and perhaps in mystery
religions. As such, they can be labelled proto-Gnostics.

How did the author counter these fallacies? First of all,
he assumed the name of 'Paul', that is, he claims apostolic
authority in so far as he is speaking from within the
authentic Pauline tradition of his community. He does not
cite Scripture frequently, though he sees it as being
inspired and useful to combat errors in 2Tim 3:16–17. The
unusual formula *pistos ho logos* in 1Tim 1:15 and Tit 3:8
refers to the kerygma; in 2Tim 2:11 to a doctrinal cultic
hymn; in 1Tim 4:9 it brings to mind the hope of the
believers; and 1Tim 3:1 it is a common tenet. It is evident,
however, that the most frequent appeal of the Pastorals is
to the liturgy. The *lex orandi* becomes the *lex credendi*
through fragments of hymns, confessions and doxologies
in 1Tim1:12–17; 2:5s; 3:16; 6:11–16; 2Tim 1:10: 2: 8,
11–13; Tit 2:11–14 and 3:4–7.

If the community wants to remain within the faith,
therefore, it must first of all treasure the *depositum fidei*
(1Tim 6:20s) bequeathed by Paul, heed the inspired Scriptures, and draw the right conclusions from their common

prayers which teach them what to believe. To err from this path is to lose one's way. If these are simple errors there is time for correction, but disobedience and perseverance lead to separation from the community and the loss of Christian identity. One treads outside the dynamic zone of the Spirit and enters that of Satan (1 Tim 1:20; 4:1).

Lastly, we must turn to the turbulent situation of the Johannine communities which furnishes us with clear criteria by which to distinguish orthodoxy from error, heresy and schism. Among the various reconstructions of the Johannine Churches, one may consider Raymond Brown's proposals in *The Community of the Beloved Disciple*[10] and his commentaries on John and his epistles in the *Anchor Bible* as generally reliable.

If we read the Gospel of John in the context in which it was composed, around the year 90, we find many passages that refer to controversies that the community had with the surrounding world: first of all, with 'the world' itself in its negative sense, that is, those who refused to acknowledge Jesus as Christ and Son of God. The world is primarily the unbelieving Jews, but also those who are blind to spiritual values. Texts like 1:20 and 3:28, which emphasise Jesus' superiority to John, point to certain groups, like those in Acts 19:1–7, who still thought that John the Baptist was the Messiah. It seems that it was not difficult to convince them of the contrary. Then there were some Jews, symbolised by Nicodemus, who were crypto-Christians (cf. 9:22–28; 12:42–43) but afraid to acknowledge Christ because of the 'excommunication' from the synagogue implicit in the twelfth blessing of the *birkat ha-minim*.[11] Lastly, there were also some Jews who had believed but were untrustworthy, 'but Jesus on his part would not entrust himself to them, because he knew all people and needed no one to testify about anyone, for he himself knew what was in everyone' (2:24; cf. 7:3–5; 8:31).

In the end of the discourse on the bread from heaven in 6:59–70 we read that 'when many of his disciples heard it, they said: 'This teaching is difficult; who can accept it? ... Because of this many of his disciples turned back and would no longer go about with him'. It is then 'the twelve' (the only time they are mentioned) who confess Jesus through the mouth of Peter. In Johannine terminology 'no longer to go about with Jesus' means to leave the community and walk out into the night, as Judas, (John 13:30), the prototype of traitors, did (6:64–65,70). This passage may refer to certain Docetists mentioned by Ignatius:[12] 'They keep away from the Eucharist and from prayer, because they do not acknowledge that the Eucharist is the flesh of our Lord Jesus Christ, which suffered for our sins, and which the Father, in his goodness, raised again'. The narrative may also refer to certain Jewish Christians who celebrated the Eucharist with water alone as they were averse to blood sacrifices.[13]

This would find confirmation in 1John 5:6–9 when the crisis in the community became more acute. The redemptive aspect of the Incarnation seems to be more stressed than Jesus' death in the gospel, and the people to whom Ignatius refers would have either devalued or denied the sacrificial aspect of Christ's death: 'This the one who came by water and blood, Jesus Christ, not with water only, but with water and blood'. The emphasis on blood points to a devaluation of the Eucharist in relation to baptism—hence an insufficient understanding of Jesus' sacrificial death. 1John 4:10 is quite clear on this matter: 'In this is love, not that we loved God but that he loved us and sent his Son to be the atoning sacrifice for our sins'. The Incarnation, therefore, includes Christ's sacrifice.

It follows that 'the Presbyter' had to battle on two fronts: against those who did not confess Christ as the Son of God, probably a hard-core of Jewish Christians, and Docetic tendencies that would not acknowledge a Christ who came in the flesh. This time, however, it was not a question of simple, easily correctable error. A schism had taken place: 'They went out from us, but they did not belong to us; for if they had belonged to us, they would have remained with us' (1Jn 2:19). In the preceding verse they are said to be a sign that the Antichrist is already in this world, a 'world' to which they belong and by which they are applauded (1Jn 4:5). They are no longer in communion with God (2Jn 9) because they follow the steps of their prototype, Judas. They should be kept away. A certain Diotrephes would not even receive the Presbyter's envoys. He spoke badly of this authority and expelled from the Church those who were in his favour.

The discord becomes more complicated because the secessionists appeal to the spirit of prophecy (2:18; 4:1–6). However, as in 1Cor 12:2, a prophecy cannot be genuine if it contradicts the confession that Christ came in the flesh. The community had its usual fundamentalists as well as its progressives 'who do not abide in the teaching of Christ but go beyond it' (cf. 2Jn 9).

These were the problems that faced John and/or the Presbyter. Which theological principles does he use to keep his flock together and immune to error? The first appeal is to 'what was from the beginning', the earliest preaching the community heard and still the foundation of its faith. We also find this in the opening of John's Gospel, the Logos hymn (1:1–4). But while the accent in this prologue is laid on the divinity of Christ, who was made flesh, the prologue to the First Letter of John stresses his humanity: 'We declare to you what was from the beginning, what we have heard,

what we have seen with our eyes, what we have looked at
and touched with our hands, [as Thomas did] concerning
the word of life' (1:1; 2:13, 24; 3: 11; 2Jn 5). The response to
the kerygma is the confession of faith: 'No one who denies
the Son has the Father; everyone who confesses the Son has
the Father also. Let what you heard from the beginning
abide in you' (1Jn 2:13).

This recalls Paul's appeal to the Corinthians (1Cor 12),
some of whom, as in John's case, had invoked the Spirit of
prophecy: 'Beloved, do not believe every spirit, but test the
spirits to see whether they are from God; for many false
prophets have gone out into the world. By this you know
the Spirit of God: everyone that confesses that Jesus Christ
has come in the flesh is from God, and every spirit that
does not confess Jesus is not from God. And this is the
spirit of the Antichrist' (1Jn 4:1–4).

It is not these people that have the Spirit of God; it is the
faithful who possess the true Spirit, for the anointing with
which they have been marked is their internal teacher in the
sense of Jer 31:34 and John 6:45: 'they shall by taught by God'.
'You have been anointed by the Holy One, and all of you have
knowledge' (2:20). This is what we call the *sensus fidelium*—
that instinct which spontaneously reacts with distrust to
every assertion that does not reflect the habitual confession.
It is quite natural that the secessionists, whether Hellenistic
or Jewish, are loved by 'the world' because they speak its
language (1Jn 3:3). They may indeed be loved by the world,
but their dissension is a sin against the love that binds
together the *koinonia*—John's equivalent of orthodoxy.

The commonwealth of *koinonia* in which the Spirit
testifies is the community of the baptised who commem-
orate Christ's death in the Eucharist: 'And the Spirit is the
one that testifies, for the Spirit is the truth. There are three

that testify: the Spirit and the water and the blood, and these three agree' (1Jn 5: 6–7).

We have observed that in John 6:60 Jesus turns to 'the Twelve' against those who no longer went about with him, and it is Peter who professes his and their adherence to Jesus. This is a sign of the loyalty of John's community to apostolic authority and to Peter. The letters in Rev 2 and 3 may illustrate the situation in which the recipients of the epistles found themselves.

Apart from the first century writings that would later belong to the canon, there are some contemporary documents that can complete our search for criteria. The oldest is perhaps the so-termed Didache. It begins with the 'two ways' doctrine; the ways of good and wicked behaviour (1:1), based on Jewish tradition and on 'the works of the flesh and the works of the Spirit' in Gal 5. The list is taken up by Barnabas and seems to have belonged to the traditional catechesis in early Christianity, being inherited from Judaism. The book warns sternly against schism (4:3), as do 1Clem (*passim*) and Barn 19:12. The Didache also provides some practical rules on how false apostles or prophets can be discerned.[14]

1Clement was written by the Roman Church to reprimand the Corinthian congregation about its divisions over the election of certain presbyters. It does so with some authority. Clement points to the constancy of the martyrs (5:1) as a model of behaviour. The gospel, of course, is that of Jesus Christ, the Master, who received it from God and handed it over to the apostles (42:1; Cf. Barn 5:8). The letter quotes lavishly from the Old Testament, inspired by the Holy Spirit (45:1; 53:1), as he himself feels he is in writing the letter (63:2).

Ignatius' main emphasis is on the unity of the Church with the monarchic bishop, the priests and deacons. Eph

9:1 praises the recipients for blocking their ears to people who had tried to spread errors among them. They resisted through their faith, that is, the tradition implicit in their *sensus fidei*. In Magnesians 8:1 Ignatius makes an interesting statement: he tells Judaisers that it is not Christianity that is founded on Judaism, but Judaism on Christianity, because the Prophets had believed in Jesus Christ. He, too, feels that he is proclaiming prophecy (Philadelphians 7:1); and in 8:2, writing about some people who would not believe anything that was not written in 'the archives' (probably the OT), he states that his archive is Jesus Christ himself, his death and resurrection.

It is now time to draw some conclusions from the above analysis. We will give a list of all the criteria we have found in the various writings examined. It is obvious that these criteria are scattered here and there, but they are indicative of the discussions within the Churches that underlie the written documents themselves. We shall see in the following chapters how the Fathers adopted them and developed them in the context of their theological discussions.

The criteria are the following: appeal to the Lord, to the kerygma, to confessions of faith, to apostolic authority, to the Scriptures, to the traditions left by the founders, to a 'Council', to the *depositum fidei,* to the *lex orandi,* and to the *sensus fidelium,* to genuine charismatic prophecy, to the witness of the martyrs, and to the signs of the Spirit in the missions. It is essential to preserve the *koinonia,* hence the avoidance of divisions and schism. This would be the task of the bishops. Perhaps we can also speak of the Petrine mandate (Matthew and John) and of the Roman Church (1Clem).

Orthodoxy, therefore, is preserved by perseverance in faith in Christ, Son of Man and Son of God, as laid down by the apostolic founders of the Churches, nurtured and developed by the Holy Spirit. Whatever diverges from this tradition can lead into error, and, when there is persever- ance in error, into heresy and schism.

Notes

1. C. H. Dodd, *The Apostolic Preaching and its Developments* (London, 1936). P. Grech, 'Tradition and Theology in Apostolic Times', in *A New Catholic Commentary on Holy Scripture* (1969), pp. 665–700. Further attempts to find a core NT kerygma were those of P. Carrington, *The Primitive Christian Catechism* (Cambridge, 1949) and A. Seeberg, *Der Katechismus der Urchristenheit* (Munich, 1966).
2. E. Käsemann, *Exegetische Versuche und Besinnungen* (Tübingen, 1960).
3. Cf. P. Grech, 'Il kerigma della comunità giovannea' and 'Le confessioni di fede in Giovanni' in *Il messaggio biblico e la sua interpretazione* (Bologna, 2005), pp. 333–342; 343–350.
4. E. E. Lemcio, *The Past of Jesus in the Gospels* (Cambridge, 1991).
5. See V. Neufeld, *The Earliest Christian Confessions* (Leiden, 1963).
6. Our knowledge of the Ebionites is mainly based on the reconstruction of the Pseudo-Clementine literature. It is interesting to compare Epiphanius' account of them in *The Panarion of St. Epiphanius Bishopè of Salamis* (Oxford, 1990), pp. 94–107 with the Jewish point of view in H.-J., Schoeps, *Theologie und Geschichte des Judenchristentums* (Tübingen, 1949). More recent is S. C. Mimouni, *Les chrétiens d'origine juive dans l'antiquité* (Paris, 2004), pp. 159–194.
7. Cf. J. Sanders, *Schismatics, Sectarians, Dissidents, Deviants* (London, 1993).
8. P. Grech, 'L'apologia di Paolo negli Atti degli Apostoli' in *Ermeneutica e teologia biblica* (Rome, 1986), pp. 397–410.
9. A. T. Hanson, *The Pastoral Epistles (The New Century Bible Commentary)* (Grand Rapids, 1982), pp. 28–31. Some authors still insist on the Pauline authenticity of the Pastorals: G. W. Knight III, *The Pastoral Epistles* (Grand Rapids, 1992).
10. R. E. Brown, *The Community of the Beloved Disciple: The Life, Loves and Hates of an Individual Church in New Testament Times*

(London, 1979). See also G. M. Burge, *The Anointed Community: The Holy Spirit in the Johannine Tradition* (Grand Rapids, 1987).

11. *Min* is an unorthodox Jew rather than a 'heretic'. The Palestinian version added the *Nosrim* (Nazareans), i.e., the Christians, probably those who did not observe the Torah.

12. St Ignatius of Antioch, *Letter to the Smyrnians*, 7:2.

13. St Epiphanius, *Panarion*, 30,16,1; St Irenaeus, *Adversus haereses*, 4:13.

14. *Didache* 11–13.

2 FORMULATING CHRISTIAN SELF-IDENTITY

S ELF-DEFINITION IS THE formulation of self-awareness in regard to oneself and to others. The first half
of the second century was crucial for Christians in
clarifying their own identity to themselves and to the
surrounding gentile and Jewish context.

Around the end of the first century, when the Gospel
and Epistles of John had just appeared, some of the other
letters had not yet been written, but the Christ-believers
were spread around the Mediterranean, each Church
following the tradition of its founder. They were united
by baptism and faith in Jesus Christ, Son of Man and Son
of God. Their specific cult was the celebration of the Lord's
Supper. The Bible they read was the Septuagint Old
Testament whose God they worshipped and with reference to whose prophecies they interpreted the person, life,
death and resurrection of Jesus. Yahweh is now the Father,
or the Father of our Lord (*Kyrios*) Jesus Christ. Their
biblical interpretation was inherited from Judaism, though
it is not wrong to say that it was closer to the Alexandrian
tradition. But Scripture was now read in a new interpretative Christological key. The four Gospels began to
circulate rapidly, while the letters were read in the
Churches to which they had been addressed, and eagerly
requested by other Churches.

Though a clean separation of Church from Synagogue
was still far away, Christians as a group were often—
though not always—seen by Jews as outsiders. Justin's
Dialogue with Trypho, however, makes it clear that both

Jews and Christians were well aware of the doctrinal chasm that divided them. As to their distinction from the pagan world, Jews and Christians were on the same side. The early Christian apologetic writers joined forces with traditional Greek Jewish literature to assert their right as an established religion.

In the preceding chapter we spoke of brief but clear confessions of faith in Christ in response to the kerygma. These coalesced later to form the rule of faith, and, later still, the creeds.[1] We find the expression *kanon tes paradoseos hemon* in 1 Clement,[2] but not yet in its full technical sense. It was Irenaeus who expounded its full meaning a few decades later.

Before the maturation of the *regula fidei*, however, Christians expressed the essence of their belief in their answers to the baptismal interrogations. The rite was administered in the name of the Father and of the Son and of the Holy Spirit (in some cases in the name of Christ), and this rite of initiation provided the occasion for a full acknowledgment of their Christian identity. The confession could be declaratory or interrogative. In the *Apostolic Tradition*,[3] formerly preserved under the name of Hippolytus, the baptismal rite is described fully. The presbyter made a clear interrogation to which the neophyte answered "I believe". He professed his faith in the Father Almighty, in Christ Jesus, the Son of God, who was born of the Holy Spirit, from the Virgin Mary, was crucified under Pontius Pilate, was buried, rose again on the third day, alive from the dead, ascended into heaven, and sat at the right hand of the Father, about to come to judge the living and the dead. The profession ended with faith in the Holy Spirit and the holy Church and the resurrection of the flesh.

This Roman ritual, dating from about 200 CE, is probably a developed form of simpler rites that go back to the earliest times. In this way, the baptised person defined himself or herself as belonging to a religion that recognised God as Father, Son and Holy Spirit. The centrality of the historical figure of Jesus the Christ, his suffering, death, burial and resurrection, left little or no space for a Docetic understanding of Jesus. Christian eschatology is also clearly outlined.

The confession marked out the Christians as distinct from Jews and pagans. The *regula fidei*, or rule of faith, is not a solemn ritual and public declaration of faith. It is a positive, theological summary of what forms the backbone of a developing Christian tradition. It keeps together all Christians scattered among the several Churches. When it merged with the baptismal confession, it gave birth to the various creeds.

As we said above, the first full statement of the rule of faith is to be found in Irenaeus' *Adversus haereses* as well as in his *Epideixis.*[4] It deserves to be quoted in full as it is the archetype of future references to the Rule:

> For the Church, although dispersed throughout the whole world even to the ends of the earth, has received from the apostles and from their disciples the faith in one God, Father Almighty, the Creator of heaven and earth and sea and all that is in them; and in the one Jesus Christ, the Son of God, who became flesh for our salvation; and in the Holy Spirit, who announced through the prophets the dispensations and the comings, and the birth from a Virgin, and the passion, and the resurrection from the dead, and the bodily ascension into heaven of the beloved Christ Jesus our Lord, and his coming from heaven in the glory of the Father to re-establish all things; and the raising up again of all flesh of all humanity, in order that to Jesus Christ our Lord and God and Saviour and King, in

accord with the approval of the invisible Father
every knee shall bend of those in heaven and on
earth and under the earth, and every tongue shall
confess him, and that he may make just judgment
of them all; and that he may send the spiritual
forces of wickedness, and the angels who trans-
gressed and became apostates, and the impious,
unjust, lawless and blasphemous among men, into
everlasting fire; and that he may grant life, immor-
tality, and surround with eternal glory the just and
the holy, and those who have kept his commands
and who have persevered in his love, either from
their beginning or from their repentance.

Apart from the positive contents of this paragraph, it is
certainly coloured with a tinge of anti-Gnostic controversy, about which we shall speak later. However, strictly
related to the Rule of Faith was the interpretation of
Scripture. Irenaeus accuses the Gnostics of extrapolating
a biblical phrase from its context to interpret it within their
own philosophical principles.[5] He therefore lays down a
few rules for a correct explanation of the true sense of the
Scriptures. First of all a phrase must be interpreted in its
immediate literary context, the 'sentence' or 'paragraph'
to which it belongs, thus revealing the author's intention.
He gives the example of some authors who chose phrases
from Homer, stitched them together and claimed that
Homer was of their opinion. This is what the Gnostics
were doing with the Bible. Secondly, the interpretative
context should include the whole Bible, the Old and New
Testaments.[6] The Scriptures have one author, the one
God, who is the God of both Testaments. Hence Scripture
cannot contradict itself.[7] And, lastly, the context of a true
Christian interpretation is the Rule of Faith described
above. One could object, of course, that inserting a biblical
saying into an *a priori* rule would be as mistaken as the

Gnostics were accused of being. Our author would reply that the *regula fidei* is nothing else but a synthesis of biblical faith transmitted publicly by the bishops and that it forms part of the apostolic tradition in which the Christian faith has its origins.

Clement of Alexandria adds another dimension to Irenaeus' three contexts—that of symbolic reason, which opens the way to dialogue with the Hellenistic world and endows the universe with a sacramental power. But he, too, insists on the Rule as well. He calls it the 'ecclesiastical rule', received from those who taught him, perhaps Tatian, Theodosion and Pantaenus. He defines it as 'The concord and harmony of the law and the prophets delivered at the coming of the Lord'.[8]

That Origen stressed the Rule of Faith comes to us as a surprise. We may recall that his writings were banned by the Second Council of Constantinople, perhaps due to erroneous interpretations. However, in the preface of his *De principiis* he makes the distinction between doctrines that are accepted as certain, belonging to the Rule of Faith, and others that are still open to research and discussion. In Origen's time the Rule was more or less as it had been formulated by Irenaeus. A century later the Council of Nicaea, with all the preceding and subsequent theological discussions, clarified, broadened and standardised the tenets that belonged to the faith. Indeed, so much so that Rufinus, who translated *On First Principles* into Latin, writes in his own preface that he would leave out those sections—so dear to Origen—that were contrary to the Rule. Indeed when in *De principiis* IV, 2, the Alexandrian theologian explains the criteria for the correct interpretation of Scripture and the use of allegory, he openly states: 'And we shall try to make clear what seems to us the right way of understanding Scripture, observing that rule and

discipline which was delivered by Jesus Christ to the
apostles and which they deliver in succession to their
followers who teach the heavenly Church'. Any subsequent criticism of Origen, therefore, does not weaken his
position as a witness to the validity of the Rule of Faith as
a criterion of biblical interpretation.

Moving west from Alexandria to Carthage, we meet the
first Latin writer, Tertullian, whose witness to the *regula*
is even stronger than that of Irenaeus'. Indeed, he was
sometimes reproached for belittling Scripture in favour of
the Rule of Faith. This was not the case, however. The true
reason was that in *De praescriptione*, which was mainly
written against the Gnostics, he warns the faithful that
these 'heretics' play around so much with biblical texts
that it would be safer to hold fast to the Rule of Faith than
let oneself be confused by so much juggling. The Rule is
found in all the apostolic Churches, and in all other
Churches that hold the same faith, for universality of belief
and antiquity of doctrine converge in their witness to
apostolic origin, and, in the last resort, to Christ's teaching.
It is only within this context that the Scriptures should be
read. Tertullian expounds the Rule in 13:1:

> There is only one God, and none other besides him;
> the creator of the world, who brought forth all
> things out of nothing, though his Word first of all
> sent forth; this Word is called his Son; and in the
> name of God he was seen at various times by the
> Patriarchs, and has always been heard in the
> Prophets; and at last he was brought down from
> the Spirit and Power of God the Father into the
> virgin Mary, and was made flesh in her womb, and
> having been born from her, came forth as Jesus
> Christ. Thenceforth he preached a new law and a
> new promise of the Kingdom of Heaven; worked
> miracles; was crucified, rose again on the third day;

and having ascended into heaven sat at the right of the Father; sent the Holy Spirit with vicarious power to lead those who believe; is going to come in glory to take the saints into the enjoyment of eternal life and of the heavenly promises, and to condemn the godless to eternal fire, after the resurrection of both classes and their restoration in the flesh. This rule, as will be proved, was taught by Christ, and admits no questions among us, except those which heresies bring in and which make them heretics.

In *De virginibus velandis* 1:3 the African writer adds: 'The law of faith remaining the same, the other points of discipline and practice admit newer correction, since, of course, the grace of God works and perfects up to the end'. This addition is important because it implies that the Rule is not static: it can grow, with the help of the Spirit, in points of ecclesiastical discipline and liturgical practice. Tradition, therefore, is extended to include ritual, but this is subject to change only if it does not contradict the backbone of the Rule of Faith. Peter and Paul, too, had their altercations but they agreed on the one faith; the latter asserts that many preach Christ with insincere intention, but it is always the true Christ who is preached.

The validity of the *lex orandi* as testimony to the *lex credendi* is later taken up by Basil who in *De Spiritu Sancto* XXVII enumerates diverse liturgical practices accepted by the Church, of which, however, there is no written record. These, he states, derive from the oral and private teaching of the apostles, inherited through tradition by the Church. Fortunately, the days of the Gnostic controversy were over, otherwise the argument would have been two-edged. But as baptismal confessions of faith obtain a special place in Basil's book, and these are not explicitly prescribed in the New Testament, we can understand very well what he meant. Tradition does not limit itself to the Church's faith and preaching—it includes all its practices and way of life. This is the true context of the written word which has the self-same apostolic authority as its source.[9] What was essential, therefore, was the *kyriakon* and *apostolikon*. Scripture and tradition were the two channels through which to reach this source. Scripture, of course, was considered inspired and the main foundation of the Rule of Faith, within which, however, it had to be interpreted. The Holy Spirit guided both of them.

In the meanwhile, the creeds were being formulated. The Rule of Faith recited by Irenaeus, Clement, Origen and Tertullian—one in substance but differing in its length and expression—now loses its flexibility and crystallises into the several creedal formulations following the Arian controversies.[10] As we shall see later, Augustine sees them as a synthesis of biblical theology, but they are much more than that. As we saw above, baptism, from the very first decades of the second century, was accompanied by a profession of faith, whether interrogatory or declaratory, related to the Rule of Faith. Around 330, however, after Nicaea, the Roman Church formulated a symbol, founded on a second-century Greek creed, which then gave rise to the Apostles' Creed that was accepted in the West in the ninth century. The Council of Nicaea also formulated a creed, which, according to Eusebius, was in accordance with the one he had professed at baptism, with the addition of some anti-Arian phrases. After some subsequent experimental attempts at codifying other professions, the Council of Constantinople in 381 drew up the final form of the Constantinopolitan Creed,[11] in which process the Cappadocian fathers played no small part. Later, the Latin symbol known as *Quicumque*, probably stemming from Augustinian sources in North Africa, came into being. This is important for our subject because the next witness to the Rule, exemplary in his completeness, is specifically Augustine. We shall dwell a little longer on this because he can be called the theologian of the *regula fidei,* which he mentions as *regula pietatis, regula ecclesiastica, regula veritatis* or *analogia fidei* about one hundred times. He incorporates all that had been said about it earlier, adding his own observations. According to the Bishop of Hippo, the Rule was laid down by Christ and the apostles.[12] It was the fulfilment of what Jesus had promised in John 16:12—that the Paraclete would complete the teaching he himself could not give during his lifetime;[13] and of Gal 1: 6 regarding apostolic authority.[14] It had been handed down by Christians of old who had scrutinised the Scriptures.[15] Its antiquity was a pledge against heretical doctrinal innovations.[16]

We said above that by Augustine's time the Rule of Faith had been expanded to include recent convictions arrived at by the consent of the universal Church. What doctrines, then, did the Bishop of Hippo's ecclesiastical rule comprise, or, better, which were its sources? It is evident that Scripture occupies the first place; but as biblical misinterpretation also can be a begetter of heresy, he follows Irenaeus by saying that interpretation should begin with the clearer and more certain texts, not with the more obscure ones.[17]

The Rule received at baptism is the Creed. It is a compendium of biblical doctrine. Which creed, however? We would be tempted to say that after 381 we have both the Nicene and Constantinopolitan confessions, but these formulations were not adopted as baptismal creeds in the West until later. Augustine himself comments on the baptismal symbol in *Sermo* 215. J.N.D. Kelly reconstructs the Hippo creed as follows:

> *Credimus in Deum Patrem omnipotentem, univer-*
> *sorum creatorem, regem saeculorum, immortalem*
> *et invisibilem. Credimus et in Filium eius Jesum*
> *Chrstum Dominum nostrum, natum de Spirtu*
> *Sancto ex virgine Maria, crucifixum sub Pontio*
> *Pilato, mortuum et sepultum, (qui) tertia die*
> *resurrexit a mortuis, ascendit ad coelos, sedet ad*
> *dexteram Dei Patris, inde venturus est iudicare*
> *vivos et mortuos. Credimus et in Spiritum Sanctum,*
> *remissionem peccaturum, resurrectionem carnis,*
> *vitam aeternam per sanctam ecclesiam.*

We find cognate confessions in Carthage and Ruspe as well; but even creeds can be misinterpreted. There are people, says Augustine, who recite the words of the creed but twist their meaning to suit their own errors.[18] Moreover, the creed does not contain anything about recent controversies—original sin, for example.[19] It, too, therefore, needs supporting external evidence which this bishop finds in the liturgical rites and in the *lex orandi*. The ancient and universal custom of baptising infants is adduced as a belief in the inheritance of Adam's sin. And as official prayers cannot contain any error, they can be relied upon to interpret the true faith of Christians.

Augustine also appeals to the universal testimony of the ancient Fathers and bishops whose writings he commends to young people for their rhetoric. In *Contra Iulianum*,[20] John of Constantinople and his fellow bishops, Innocent of Rome, Ambrose of Milan, Cyprian of Carthage, Basil of Cappadocia, and Hilary of Gaul, are called upon as witnesses against Pelagian teachings. There are, it is true, points of theological disagreement even among these Fathers, but they all agree on the essence of faith. He attributes the soundest authority to the plenary councils to buttress his own theses.[21] The frequent appeals of the African bishops to Rome point to their veneration for the see occupied by Peter's successors.

In addition, we cannot neglect Augustine's respect for the *sensus fidelium*. He makes ample use of Phil 3:16–17: 'Let those who are mature be thus minded; and if anything you are otherwise minded, God will reveal that also to you. Only let us hold true to what we have attained'. God had 'revealed' the Rule of Faith to his mother Monica, for example.[22] The simple faithful, however, have this rule to guide them until God reveals to them things spiritual as long as they do not dogmatise their unhealthy opinions and are willing to be corrected by ecclesiastical authority. He himself confesses that he is unable to answer the question why God, according to Wisdom 4:11, does not take away from this world those who are about to sin and lose His grace.[23] He does give a provisional answer and allows for other opinions as long as they stand within the framework of the Rule of Faith, until God reveals better answers. Even the rule itself sometimes requires one *distinguo* or other to be understood correctly. The learned themselves should follow the *regula* as taught by the more humble. In fact, it is not enough to remain within this rule if one, like the nine healed lepers, does not render thanks to God. So, says Augustine, construct upon the foundations of this rule, without adding, subtracting or doubting, and God will add further revelation. Everyone's understanding of the Rule of Faith is given according to the measure of each person's faith in order to provoke the mind to delve deeper into God's mysteries.

Lastly, we must ask how Augustine's notion of the Rule of Faith affected his interpretation of Scripture. His hermeneutical methods are to be found in books 2 and 3 of *De doctrina Christiana*, of which, for obvious reasons, we can only provide the barest tenets, limiting ourselves

to those passages that need ecclesiastical doctrine to
interpret them. It should also be clear that the bishop who
preached to his congregation in the basilica of Hippo is
much freer in his interpretation than when he composes
De Trinitate and when he argues against Julian. There is
a spiritual pastoral explanation of biblical texts as well as
a strictly theological one. Sometimes a homily can just
contain a reflection on a subject rather than the explanation of a text.

The strictly exegetical method can be summed up in a
few rules: the proper meaning of a text is what the human
author intended to say in his social and historical circumstances.[24] Attention should be paid to the 'separation of
words', a necessary practice when manuscripts did not
separate one word from another and contained no punctuation. If the separation is not clear, it is *a priori* erroneous if it contradicts the Rule of Faith.[25] If there is an
alternative reading within Catholic doctrine, then the
literary context should be taken into account and this
applies to punctuation as well.[26] Furthermore, if your
manuscript offers no difficulty and the translation is
correct, yet the meaning is counter to the faith, then your
understanding is mistaken. Moreover, it is the rule that
determines which book is to be considered as canonical
or not, for the apocrypha do not only contain unhistorical
narratives but sometimes offend against the faith as well.
If the literal sense of the text is orthodox, hold on to it.[27]
Differences of interpretation within the limits of faith are
all acceptable, even if they are merely figurative. If an Old
Testament verse is interpreted by some New Testament
writer, then that is its real meaning. Figurative exegesis,
however, should always retain a certain analogy with the
literal meaning to prevent it becoming mere fancy. A
wrong interpretation of difficult texts in Scripture can be

a source of error, so the reader should either admit his inability to understand or propose an interpretation within the Rule. Augustine himself was baffled by such texts as 'When I was with them' in John 17:12, 'The Father is greater than I' (Jn 14:28), and Paul's explanation of Adam's sin in Rom 5:12–20, but he would not dare explain them in a way that was contrary to contemporary doctrine accepted as certain.[28] He was, therefore, more concerned about an orthodox explanation than he was about a literally exact one because he was convinced that the former would at least not be a false one though it might not give the exact rendering.

All this will seem ridiculous to a modern biblical scholar accustomed to the critical-historical method, as there would be no progress if we only stick to the catechism. It must be admitted, however, that few modern theologians, or exegetes for that matter, have never dipped their pen into Augustine's commentaries, especially those on the Psalms and on John's writings. A dialogue between the Church's faith and scientific exegesis is helpful to both.

From what we have said, it should be evident that the *regula fidei*, by Augustine's time, had assumed a much broader dimension than it had had in Irenaeus' time. It comprised all those doctrines where the universal Church had attained certainty, basing its development on a better understanding of Scripture, on the creeds, the councils, traditional liturgical practice and the faith of more mature Christians.

Notes

1. See P. Grech, 'The Regula Fidei as Hermeneutical Principle Yesterday and Today' in *Il messaggio biblico e la sua interpretazione* (Bologna, 2005), pp. 147–162; J. N. D. Kelly, *Early Christian Creeds*, third edition (New York, 1972).
2. Pope St Clement I, *First Letter to the Corinthians*, 7,2; 4,1.

3. *Apostolic Tradition,* 21.
4. St Irenaeus, *Adversus haereses,* 1,10,1; *Epideixis* 3 and 6.
5. St Irenaeus, *Adversus haereses,* 1,9,4.
6. *Ibid.,* 3,6,1.
7. *Ibid.,* 1,9,4.
8. Clement of Alexandria, *Stromata,* 7,16; 6,15; 1,1.
9. Cf. Vatican II, *Dei Verbum,* 8.
10. See L. H. Westra, *The Apostles' Creed: Origin, History and some Early Commentaries* (Turnhout, 1992).
11. The text of this creed is only preserved in the acts of the Council of Chalcedon.
12. St Augustine, *Epistula* 265,6.
13. St Augustine, *In Iohannis evangelium tractatus,* 98,7.
14. St Augustine, *Enarrationes in Psalmos,* 115,1.
15. *Ibid.,* 10,8.
16. St Augustine, *Contra Jiulianum opus imperfectum* 11,22.
17. St Augustine, *Quaestiones in Heptateuchum* 5,29.
18. St Augustine, *De baptismo contra donatistas* 3,4,9.
19. *Ibid.,* 6,25,47.
20. St Augustine, *Contra Iulianum,* I,7,30–31.
21. *Ibid.*
22. St Augustine, *Confessions* VIII,12.
23. St Augustine, *Epistula* 217,4.
24. St Augustine, *Sermo* 7,45.
25. St Augustine, *De doctrina Christiana.* III,2.
26. *Ibid.*
27. St Augustine, *Epistula* 147,14.
28. St Augustine, *De nuptiis et concupiscentia* I,1,1.

3 THE APOSTOLIC TRADITION

THE RULE OF Faith and the apostolic tradition are so closely intertwined that they are often indistinguishable from one other. The difference seems to be that whereas the *regula fidei* forms the backbone of that faith essential to Christian identity, the traditions that are considered of apostolic origin comprise broader theological discussions, which, when mature enough to reach certainty, may flow into the mainstream of faith and enter the creeds.

Willy Rordorf and André Schneider published an excellent anthology of patristic texts about the apostolic tradition in their book *Die Entwicklung des Traditionsbegriff in der Alten Kirche* on which we shall base our enquiry.[1]

This time we shall begin at the very end by quoting an extract from Vincent of Lerins, in whom the patristic theology of tradition reached its maturity. We shall then proceed chronologically to understand how Vincent arrived at this *classic* synthesis:

> And thus, because of so many distortions of such various errors, it is highly necessary that the line of prophetic and apostolic interpretation be directed in accord with the norm of the ecclesiastical and Catholic meaning. In the Catholic Church herself every care must be taken that we may hold fast to that which has been believed everywhere, always and by all, for this is, then, truly and properly Catholic. That is what the force and meaning of the name itself declares, a name that embraces all almost universally. This general rule will be

correctly applied if we pursue universality, antiquity and agreement. And we follow universality in
this way, if we confess this one faith to be true,
which is confessed by the whole Church throughout the whole world; antiquity, however, if we in
no way depart from those interpretations which,
it is clear, our whole predecessors and fathers
solemnised; and likewise agreement, if, in this very
antiquity, we adopt the definitions and theses of all
or certainly of almost all priests and teachers'
(*Commonitarium* 2, 1).

In the preceding chapter we had to wait until Irenaeus to
have a clear outline of the Rule of Faith. This had its roots
in the confessions of faith during the apostolic period, as
we saw in chapter one. As did tradition. In fact, many of
the Fathers make reference to texts we mentioned above,
especially 1Cor 11:2; Gal 1:8–9; 2Thess 2:15; and 1Tim
6:20–21. Other first century writings, the Didache (4:3)
and 1Clem (I Cor 7:2–3), exhort believers to hold fast to
traditions that go back to the very origins and which were
entrusted to the bishops and deacons (I Cor 42:5). With
the rise of mono-episcopacy in Ignatius' time, this role
passed to the bishops.[2]

However, it is once more with Irenaeus and Tertullian
that the argument from tradition comes to the fore,
obviously against the Gnostics. These, too, appealed to a
tradition handed down to them in secret from one apostle
or another. In fact, as we shall see later, there were many
Gnostic gospels, acts, letters and apocalypses in circulation, in the second and third centuries, bearing the name
of an immediate disciple of Christ. The situation became
more confused when Gnostics infiltrated traditional
Christian communities expressing themselves in an
ambiguous language that could also be understood in an
orthodox manner. The Bishop of Lyon studied these

phrases in their proper Gnostic context and it was he who alerted Victor, the Bishop of Rome, to the fact that his Church abounded in Gnostic or Gnosticising groups, who, wittingly or unwittingly, were straying from traditional doctrine.[3] This is what his book *Adversus haereses* is about. It is here that we must look for Irenaeus' manner of discerning what he held to be authentic apostolic traditions, understood in their proper context, from analogous ones belonging to another frame of reference. As we shall try to sketch a simplified itinerary through the maze of Gnostic systems in the next chapter, here we limit ourselves to some generic terms.

In the previous chapter we quoted in full Irenaeus' version of the *Regula fidei*, which, he asserts, is derived from the apostles. Writing less than a century after the apostolic period, he states that it was still possible to count the succession of bishops in the various Churches founded by apostles up to his own times. He denies categorically that any secret tradition ever existed. This would otherwise have been delivered to the bishops who would have made it public.[4] Irenaeus makes special mention of Polycarp, the Bishop of Smyrna, whom he had known personally;[5] but his well-known testimony on the particular case of the Church of Rome is worth quoting in full:

> But since it would be too long to enumerate in such a volume as this the successions of all the churches, we shall confound all those who, in whatever manner, whether through self-satisfaction or vainglory, or through blindness and wicked opinion, assemble other than where it is proper, by pointing out here the succession of the bishops of the greatest and most ancient Church known to all, founded and organized at Rome by the two most glorious apostles, Peter and Paul, the Church which has the tradition and the faith which comes

> down to us after having been announced to men
> by the apostles, for with this Church, because of its
> superior origin, all Churches must agree, that is,
> all the faithful in the whole world; and it is in her
> that all the faithful everywhere have maintained
> the apostolic tradition.[6]

This is followed in *Adversus haereses* 3,3,3 by the names
of the Bishops of Rome who succeeded Peter. The last
sentence in the Latin version can mean that the faithful in
Rome have maintained the tradition or that the believers
who have poured into Rome have enriched the Church
with their faith.

It follows that all doctrinal disputes should maintain
these most ancient traditions as their point of reference.
Even if the apostles had left us no writings of their own,
the traditions they deposited would have been sufficient
to defend us from thieves and robbers[7] for the bishops
received from them the charism of truth. Those who
belong to these Churches stand firm while other groups
who assemble elsewhere should be viewed with suspicion.[8]

The Church has now spread over the whole world;
Germans, Celts, Iberians, Syrians and Libyans may speak
different languages but they all speak with one truth, with
one mouth and soul.[9] On the contrary, heretics, the
Gnostics, are of later origin and are scattered here and
there without any cohesive teaching.[10] The true gnosis is
to be found in the apostles' doctrine, in the unity of faith
of the body of Christ and in the transmission of the
authentic scriptures without addition or deletion. All are
united by the bond of love,[11] and this organism is in
constant growth, vivified by the Holy Spirit:

> That in which we have faith is a firm system directed
> to the salvation of man; and, since it has been
> received by the Church, we guard it. Constantly it

has its youth renewed by the Spirit of God, as if it
were some precious deposit in an excellent vessel;
and it causes the vessel containing it also to be
rejuvenated...In the Church God has placed apostles,
prophets and doctors, and all the other means
through which the Spirit works; in all of which none
have any part who do not conform to the Church...
For where the Church is, there is the Spirit of God;
and where the Spirit of God there the Church and
every grace. The Spirit however, is truth.[12]

This text is very important because it is the germ from
which Vincent of Lerins' thesis would later mature. It
asserts the development of doctrine with the help of the
Holy Spirit, not of doctrine alone, but also of the vessel
which contains it—the Church. It is the presence of the
Spirit in the Church, working through those who possess
special charisms, and retaining her in his truth.

We find the same doctrine in Tertullian. The title of
his great work *De praecriptione haereticorum* is a legal
expression indicating that his adversaries, the Gnostics in
particular, have not proved their case. It is we ourselves
who are the rightful heirs of the apostles' legacy. Tertullian's arguments are those of a lawyer inveighing against
his opponent. His main source is Scripture, of course, but
given the arbitrary use of biblical texts by his adversaries
his main appeal is to tradition. Tradition is what God
revealed to Christ, Christ to the apostles and the apostles
to their successors, the bishops of the various Churches
they founded.[13] These Churches may be many in number,
but 'although the churches are so many and so great, there
is but the one primitive Church of the apostles, from which
all others are derived. Thus all are primitive, all are
apostolic, because all are one. The communion of peace,
the title of brotherhood and the bond of hospitality prove

her unity, privileges which no other principle governs except the one tradition of the same sacrament'.[14]

Like Irenaeus, Tertullian refers to the geographical position of the main apostolic Churches, emphasising the Roman Church 'whence also our authority derives. How happy is that Church, on which the Apostles poured out their whole doctrine along with their blood'.[15] He therefore challenges the heretics to demonstrate historically the origin of their Churches and the succession of their line of bishops back to apostolic times. If even that were possible, however, what they teach is contrary to what was taught by the apostles. Moreover, they are divided among themselves. In opposite fashion, the Churches recently founded among Christians are also apostolic because their faith is in conformity with that of those Churches truly rooted in the apostolic period.[16]

As these heretics (the Gnostics) are not Christian, they have no right to use our Scriptures,[17] interpreted for them by the devil.[18] Marcion, for example, accepts only a spurious version of Luke, ignoring John, Mark, who was Peter's interpreter, and Paul himself, whose disciple Luke was.[19] 'Our interpretation is guided by the Paraclete, who reveals and reshapes their true meaning; it is He who leads us forward'.[20] He even guides the variety of disciplines and practices in the Churches, while keeping intact the rule of faith.[21] There is a difference between traditions that belong to the Rule of Faith and those that do not. Lastly, in Tertullian's book *Scorpiace*,[22] written in his Montanist period, the author appeals to the witness of the martyrs, whose condemnation to capital punishment is recorded in all the Roman archives.

What happens in the case of a conflict of local traditions? The first example we have is Irenaeus' mediation between Victor of Rome and Polycrates of Ephesus about the date of Easter.[23] Neither of these liturgical usages violates an essential point of faith, hence both can be preserved. The case of the long altercation between the Church of Africa under Cyprian and the Bishops of Rome, Cornelius, Lucius, and later Stephen, regarding the rebaptism of those who had been christened by heretics, is quite different.[24] The practice of rebaptism had been in use in the African Church for about half a century—enough, in Cyprian's opinion, to constitute a tradition. It was buttressed by reason, too: no man can give what he himself lacks. Stephen's firm answer *Nihil innovetur, nisi quod traditum est*—nothing is to be renewed; tradition must be followed—pointed to the much older tradition of the Church of Rome which was known to be apostolic (Cyprian, *Epist.* 74,1). Every baptism administered in the name of Christ is valid. The theological reason for this tradition would be given later by Augustine who asserted that whether Peter baptises or Judas, it is always Christ who baptises.[25]

In the preceding chapter we said that Clement of Alexandria, like Irenaeus, takes the wind from the Gnostics' sails by asserting that a genuine Gnostic is a Christian who accepts God's revelation as transmitted by the apostles. Even among the true Gnostics, however, as among the so-called ones, not all are able to understand spiritual truths in the same manner:[26] it is only the more spiritual who can do this. Origen goes further and adopts the three categories into which humans can be placed: the earthly, content with the literal sense of Scripture; the psychics, or those proficient in morality; and the spiritual, those who understand the theological or allegorical sense of the Bible. These levels, in Origen, are moral transitions, unlike those of his opponents who see these three categories as predetermined. The pagans will remain material, the spirituals are born and persevere in this category; it is only the

psychics, that is, Christians, who should wake up from
their existential slumber to be saved.[27]

As to tradition, Origen censures the Gnostics' claim to
have received their teachings from secret revelations by some
apostles;[28] but he does admit that Paul did not put in writing
all the mysteries revealed to him: the rest he delivered orally
and these belong to the public Christian tradition.[29]

We cannot enter here the current dispute about the
person of Hippolytus. In the preface of *Refutatio omnium
haeresium* the author opposes Christian tradition, based
on Scripture, guided by the Holy Spirit and transmitted
by the high priests, to the secret traditions of opponents.
The same mention of grace and the Holy Spirit that
accompany tradition to defend the faithful from error is
also to be found in the *Traditio apostolica* which is usually
associated with Hippolytus.[30]

With the end of persecution and the acknowledgment
of the Church at the time of Constantine, the argument
from tradition is now used to resolve internal theological
disputes, primarily during the Arian controversy. When
opinions differ, decisions must be taken in common. Local
councils had already taken place in Cyprian's time but
were overruled by Stephen's decision.

The Arian dispute however, was a major issue, touching
the very core of Christian faith. Only a general council
could come to a certain conclusion. The theological arguments on both sides were mainly based on Scripture,
especially whether wisdom (Logos) was created or uncre-
ated; but Scripture also needed authoritative interpretation, and this could only be based on the authority of the
Fathers. Athanasius challenges the Arians to produce a list
of those Fathers who had held their doctrine.[31] It is important to note that since ecumenical councils became a *locus
theologicus* their terminology should be examined carefully.

For example, Athanasius makes a distinction between Nicaea's wording on the date of Easter—'The following has been decided'—and its doctrine on the Logos: 'But concerning matters of faith they did not write 'It has been decided', but 'Thus the Catholic Church believes.' And thereupon they confessed how they believed. They did this in order to show that their judgment was not of more recent origin, but was in fact of apostolic times: and that what they wrote was no discovery of their own, but is simply that which was taught by the apostles'.[32]

Moreover, a letter composed by a council of ninety bishops from Egypt and Libya—among whom Athanasius—to other bishops in Africa about the Nicene declarations says: 'The bishops wrote as they did, not as men inventing phrases by themselves, but as having the witness of the fathers'.[33]

As in the case of the Rule of Faith, Basil the Great appeals to the *lex orandi,* apart from his main arguments from Scripture, to prove the divinity of the Holy Spirit. But he also adds the testimony of the martyrs as witnesses, together with that of the apostles and the Fathers.[34] It is a text worth quoting because of its reference to the *disciplina arcani,* the custom of reflecting on the mysteries in one's heart and prayer, hiding them from the uninitiated. It is to be found in his classic work *De Spiritu Sancto:*

> In the same way the apostles and fathers who, in the beginning, prescribed the Church's rites, guarded in secrecy and silence the dignity of the mysteries; for that which is blabbed in public and at random and in the public ear is no mystery at all. This is the reason for our handing on of unwritten precepts and practices: that the knowledge of our dogmas may not be neglected and held in contempt by the multitude through too great a familiarity. Dogma and kerygma are two distinct

things. Dogma is observed in silence: kerygma is
proclaimed to all the world.[35]

By then the authority of the Council of Nicaea was
indisputable, as the Councils of Ephesus and Constantinople would later be. A council defines a doctrine when
its theological foundation has reached maturity, and
Gregory of Nazianzus attributes this maturation to the
Holy Spirit, as Jesus had promised and foretold in John
14:25 and 16:12–15.[36]

The Latin Fathers did not add much to what we have
been saying. There is one point, however, that should be
clarified: the value of tradition for the self-definition of the
Catholic Church, as the Universal Church is now called, is
far from meaning that Scripture has been neglected, or that
tradition overrules the Bible. Tradition only interprets
Scripture within the historically developing context of
Christianity. Augustine's rules of interpretation listed in the
previous chapter make this clear. The nuclear *regula fidei*
we found in Irenaeus has now been watered by deep
theological thought and has flowered into the broader
definitions of the universal councils. These become dogma
and, therefore, creed. The creed which has been consigned
to the newly baptised, Augustine tells his catechumens,
should be learnt by heart, written on the heart and proffered
aloud because it contains nothing else but the teachings of
Scripture, synthesised into one formula to help negligent
Christians keep the elements of their faith in their minds.[37]

The wheel has now turned full cycle. We started this
chapter by quoting Vincent of Lerins' classic text on tradition and have seen in our survey of the Fathers' testimony
how he came to his conclusion. He has more to say,
however, and this deserves our attention. He asks: if Scripture is the basis of our faith why should we turn to tradition?
His answer is that the biblical texts allow various interpre-

tations, some of them erroneous, as was the case with the interpretations of Sabellius, Donatus, Arius, Eunonius, Apollinaris, Pelagius and others. He insists that 'the line of prophetic and apostolic interpretation be directed in accordance with the norm of the ecclesiastical and Catholic meaning'.[38] Vincent lays stress on 'what has been believed everywhere, always and by all'. Moreover in our survey we have found, as in the case of the Rule of Faith, other criteria: the *lex orandi,* the witness of the martyrs, the authority of the councils, the creeds, the role of the Spirit in the organic growth of belief that maintains its identity, and the yardstick of the tradition of the Roman Church.

This is the self-identity of the 'Catholic' Church. Some call it 'mainstream Christianity', but authenticity is not a question of majorities—in the fourth century the Arians outnumbered the Catholics in some regions, as we shall see later—it is a question of roots that are deep in the apostolic tradition.

Notes

1.   W. Rordorf and A. Schneider, *Die Entwicklung des Traditions-begriffs in der Alten Kirche* (Bern, 1983).
2.   Cf. F. A. Sullivan, SJ, *From Apostles to Bishops: The Development of the Episcopacy in the Early Church* (New York, 2001); R. Brown, *Priest and Bishop: Biblical Reflections* (London, 1970).
3.   We know this from a fragmentary letter to Victor (Harvey Vol 2, frag. xxviii, p, 457) warning him about Florinus who held Valentinian ideas.
4.   St Irenaeus, *Adversus haereses*, 3,3,1.
5.   *Ibid.,* 3,3,4.
6.   *Ibid.,* 3,3,2.
7.   *Ibid.,* 3,4,1.
8.   *Ibid.,* 4,26,2.
9.   *Ibid.,* 1,10,2.
10.   *Ibid.*

11. *Ibid.*, 4,33,8.
12. *Ibid.*, 3,24,1.
13. Tertullian, *De praescriptione haereticorum*, 21,4.
14. *Ibid.*, 2,7,9.
15. *Ibid.*, 36,3.
16. *Ibid.*, 32,1,8.
17. *Ibid.*, 37,1.
18. *Ibid.*, 40,1.
19. Tertullian, *Adversus Marcionem*, 4,5,1.
20. Tertullian, *De virginibus velandis*, 1,5.
21. *Ibid.*, 1,3.
22. Tertullian, *Liber Scorpiace (Antidote for the scorpion's sting)*, 15,3.
23. Eusebius, *Historia Ecclesiastica*, 70,9.
24. The correspondence is well documented in E. Giles, *Documents Illustrating Papal Authority: A.D. 96–454* (London, 1952), pp. 49–66.
25. St Augustine, *Contra Litteram Petiliani*, 2,69; *De unitate ecclesiae*, 58.
26. Clement of Alexandria, *Stromata*, 1,12,55,1–3; and cf. Paul, 1Cor 2:6–15.
27. Origen, *De principiis* 4,1,11; 4,2,4.
28. Origen, *Commentary on 1Cor:4,16*, fragment 19.
29. Origen, *Commentary on Romans* X,11.
30. Hippolytus, *Traditio apostolica*, 1,43.
31. St Athanasius, *Letter Concerning the Decrees of the Council of Nicaea*, 27.
32. St Athanasius, *Letter Concerning the Councils of Rimini and Seleucia*, 5.
33. See Council of Nicaea in *Patrologia graeca* 6, 1028–1048.
34. St Basil, *Hymnus Contra Sabellianos et Arium et Anomaeos*, 6.
35. St Basil, *De Spiritu Sancto* 26,66.
36. St Gregory of Nazianzus, *Oratio* 31,27.
37. St Augustine, *De Symbolo ad Catechumenos, I,1*.
38. St Vincent of Lerins, *Commonitorium* 2,1.

4 A MUTUAL MIRRORING OF CHURCH AND CANON

I T IS NOT my intention in this chapter to trace the historical formation of either the Old Testament or the New Testament canon. There are enough excellent books on the subject. My purpose is to illustrate the role of the canon, the New Testament canon especially, in the birth of Christian orthodoxy.

The word *kanon*, as is well known, means a measuring yardstick. Was there a measuring rod in ancient Christianity, and if there was, who or what determined its length? Was it merely created to keep out rival Christianities, or did it emerge from the factors that have been examined in the previous two chapters?

An analogy may help us to answer these questions. All literate peoples have their 'classics'. Shakespeare and Dante were not proclaimed classics by an act of parliament or by a literary academy. They were acknowledged as such from their very birth by their readers. They not only refined, broadened and standardised the existing language (in the case of Dante it established Tuscan as Italy's official language): they also gave a new cultural impetus to that country, raising it to a higher level. Contemporaries discovered an adequate expression of thoughts of their own which they had not been able to articulate with such clarity. These writings, therefore, served as a model for future writers to create a language that would appeal to the historical, social and cultural needs of their contemporaries. The same may be said of other forms of cultural expression: music, painting and philosophy. Collections of classic works, whether in libraries, concert halls or museums, form a sort of 'canon'.

'Religions of the Book', too, have their canons. A Muslim, a Hindu or a Buddhist would recognise their own beliefs in a reading of the Quran, the Upanishads or the sermons of Buddha. They would also admit, however, that what they were reading had been the source of their faith, even if centuries of development had modified its original meaning.

Similarly, an observant Jew would say that the Torah or the Prophets not only mirror his Jewishness but are its source as well. The same thing applies to Christians and the New Testament when it began to take shape. But the Bible of the first generation Christians was the Old Testament. Its canon had not been closed nor its text standardised, as is apparent from the divergences between the LXX and the Qumran manuscripts. This happened only during, or at the end of, the second century CE. The Jews had, of course, a number of books, 22 (or 24), which they considered to be of Divine Authority, but the possibility of adding to that number was still open, and would have happened in time had the Christians not begun to put their own writings on a par with the Law and the Prophets.

In Pharisaic circles, the Torah was interpreted through an oral *midrash* that defined their identity, as did the *midrash pesher* of the Qumran community. Christian interpretation of the Old Testament was based on recent events connected with Christ and their own Christian experiences. There had been frequent re-readings and constant reinterpretations of the Old Testament itself in the course of the transmission of texts and oracles that had to be updated to be meaningful in the light of social and religious developments in Israel's history. Christian re-reading followed this pattern but went a step further: the texts of the ancient Bible became the hermeneutic of the person of Jesus and the event of Christ. The discourse of the members of the Jesus movement was interwoven with allusions to, and phrases from, the Old Testament, which, in a way, became a Christian book.

In the meanwhile, the New Testament was taking shape. The words and deeds of Jesus, the narrative of his passion and resurrection were first transmitted orally in worship and kerygma, probably accompanied by occasional partial written memoirs. The authority on which believers based their faith was 'the Lord and the Apostles', as communicated within the various communities.

The first NT writing to appear was, however, Paul's First Letter to the Thessalonians, in around 51, followed by his subsequent epistles. The first written Gospel—that of Mark—appeared around the year 70, after the death of both Peter and Paul, and was succeeded by all the other books that made up the NT at the beginning of the second century. The fact that these books appeared in writing, however, does not mean that taken together they were recognised as a 'canon' from the outset.

A preliminary note on the formation of ancient books might be of help in understanding how collections were produced during the first century. The usual form was a number of scrolls, written on parchment and rolled around a stick, hence a *volumen,* containing a determinate number of columns and verses. These were kept in a basket and were certainly not easy to carry around for an itinerant evangelist. In the first century, the *codex* form became very common. This was a bound volume, such as we use today, usually made of papyrus which reduced the cost and made it possible for several works to be bound in a single book. Thus we have, for example, P45 containing passages from the four Gospels, and P46 with the letters of Paul, including Hebrews, both dating from around 200

CE. This helped the circulation of the Gospels in particular, but the demand for these records brought about a deterioration in the quality of the text.

We can now follow Denis Farkasfalvy's[1] suggestion that the early history of the NT canon took place in four stages: the apostolic period from the death of Jesus to the destruction of the temple in the year 70; the period of collections from 70 to Bar Kochba in 135; from 135 until Justin's time, around 165, when the rise of Gnosticism took place; and after 165—the anti-Gnostic period. This will help us to have a better understanding of the various communities of the canon.

The first phase of development, that is to say, pre-70, poses many problems. As Luke describes them in the Acts, the first years seem to have been a successful response to Peter's preaching, with thousands of conversions. Difficulties arose when some ex-Pharisees objected to Paul baptising gentiles without previous circumcision. Luke says that the question reached a compromise solution at the Council of Jerusalem after Peter had related the positive experience that he had had in the house of Cornelius. When we read the epistles to the Galatians and Second Corinthians, however, it becomes clear that events were not the plain sailing that we find in Acts. Paul found formidable adversaries among staunch Jewish Christians who tried their hardest to disrupt his mission. We can reconstruct the invective from what we know of the Ebionites as portrayed in the Pseudo-Clementines.[2] They applied to Paul the name of the arch-heretic Simon. The Ebionites declined and disappeared in the second and third centuries. No wonder, then, that after the apostle's death, as has already been observed, Paul would have risked a *damnatio memoriae* had Luke not come to his defence, revealing that his mission was supported by the constant help of the Spirit and hence had God's approval. This is the reason why the Pauline writings now belonged to the canon.

How, then, can we deem the 'Apostolic period' exemplary of pure doctrine, and what meaning would this have for the formation of the canon? In Acts 2:44–47 and 4:32–35, Luke furnishes us with an ideal picture of the early community of believers. They shared their belongings, attended the temple and broke bread in their own houses. The first Christians did not see themselves as dissociated from Israel. They were Messianic Jews who accepted Jesus as the Messiah and the Son of God who was put to death and rose from the dead. We know little or nothing about the preaching and activities of the Twelve, except what Luke tells us about Peter. The only other name mentioned is that of James. In Gal 2:9 Paul also mentions John, and calls the three who were present in Jerusalem the acknowledged pillars of the Church. These four—Paul, Cephas, James and John—represent the four currents of early Christianity: the Jewish-Christian, the Pauline, the Petrine and the Johannine, to which the gospels of Matthew, Luke, Mark and John correspond.

It is worth noting here that when we speak of apostolic traditions these do not derive nominally from this or that apostle—about whom we know very little: apostolicity is a theologoumenon rather than a linear historical factor.

What has the pre-70 period to offer concerning the canon? There were only the Pauline letters, and, perhaps, Mark; but the former had not circulated widely, given the still strong suspicion of Paul among extreme right-wing Jewish Christians. Nevertheless, this was a formative period during which the Christian community defined itself in relation both to Judaism and the pagan world. It lived on the memories and preaching of Jesus' immediate disciples which gave birth to the fundamental axiom of its beliefs based on 'the authority of the Lord and the Apostles'. This would be the deposit of faith passed on to later generations, the criterion of orthodoxy or heresy, of the doctrinal authority, or not, of any presumed apostolic script. The Church was now mainly gentile, but there was not yet any clear detachment from the Synagogue. Christians thought of themselves as the New Israel, and in the first decades were seen as Jews by Roman society. It was only in the nineties that Christians were declared unwelcome in synagogues (cf. Jn 9:22; 19:38; 20:19). And the refusal of Christians to take part in Bar Kochba's messianic war was a decisive turning point in Jewish-Christian relations.[3]

By the beginning of the second century, all of the books that today form the New Testament had been written and then circulated amongst the Churches. The period between 70 and 135 was crucial for the crystallisation of these writings into some sort of apostolic corpus. Minor collections, for example the four Gospels, Acts and the Pauline letters, were the nucleus of this corpus. In 2Pt 3:15–16 'Peter' acknowledges Paul's words of wisdom in his epistles in spite of the difficulty of their interpretation, as was the case in other 'Scriptures'. Papias is an important bridge witness because he is proud of having listened to the teaching of apostolic men, and gives us a valuable account of the composition of Matthew and Mark. Other sources indicate that Papias knew of some other books as well, but nothing about Luke and Paul.[4] Polycarp's letter to the Philippians has about a hundred allusions to half of the NT canon.

In this period between 70 and 135 there were several Christian writings in circulation. Apart from those that would not enter the New Testament there was the Didache, Ignatius' and Polycarp's letters, a part of Hermas, Papias, and 1 and perhaps 2 Clement. Why was it that only some books made it into the New Testament and others did not? It was not a question of antiquity, because the Didache, 1Clem and Ignatius, for example, were older than the Pastorals and 2Pt. Their contents were in accord with the faith professed by the congregations. The Didache claimed apostolicity as well. It is also a fact that some of the Apostolic Fathers were read in the liturgy, but as its use was limited to a few Churches this did not last for long. We must look for other reasons.

Public reading is attested to in Mark 13:14; Rev 22:18; and Col 4:16. In both Pauline and Johannine communities, prophets played a prominent role. In 1Cor 14:26–33,37–40 and in 1John 2:20 and 4:1–6 the presbyter invokes the *sensus fidelium* anointed by the Spirit and the spirit of discernment in prophetic speech, in conformity with 'what was from the beginning', as a criterion of acceptability. These charisms were still alive at the beginning of the second century and it is very likely that the recognition of certain books as authoritative depended on prophetic utterance and on the sixth sense of the faithful to perceive the presence of the Spirit in books that had some claim to the apostolic tradition. They found their faith mirrored in these writings and at the same time recognised them as being the source of their beliefs. They bore the brand of their identity.

This set of writings—we cannot speak of a 'canon' at this stage—was connected in some way with the name of an apostle on whose authority that particular Church could rely, and pass on, to other Churches. A difficulty would arise in the case of pseudonymity. If a letter suddenly appeared in the name of Paul or Peter some fifty years after their death, was it not discredited as a fake?

The phenomenon of pseudonymity is common in the Old Testament: the Psalms of David, the Wisdom of Solomon, and the 'book' of Isaiah, for example. How was

it possible for a book written over a century later than
Isaiah to be received under his name and incorporated
into earlier writings, whereas other writings, bearing the
name of Moses, Judah or Reuben, did not make it into the
Jewish canon?[5]

There must have been some sort of line of thought—call
it a school or a tradition—that carried forward the concepts and principles of their titular author: 'this is what
Paul or Peter would have said in the present circumstances'. It was a hermeneutic of an apostle's doctrine
accepted as such by the readers. There is also the possibility, in the view of some scholars, that the new letter was
woven into some surviving fragment of an apostolic
writing. This would have sufficed for it to be accepted as
authoritative because it offered an acceptable solution to
current problems.

The other sub-apostolic writings might have been
orthodox and edifying but they either lacked roots in
antiquity or their circulation was not wide enough to make
them 'catholic'.

In the first decades of the second century, however,
there was an abundance of Gnostic or Gnosticising com-
positions, in the acknowledged genres of Gospels, Acts,
Letters and the Apocalypse, circulating widely in the
Churches. We shall address this subject in the next
chapter. Here it is sufficient to say that the *sensus fidelium*
found them sinister because they not only did not ring a
bell but also contradicted accepted doctrines. The words
of the Gospel 'They will not follow a stranger, but will run
from him because they do not know the voice of strangers'
(Jn 10:5) are appropriate.

The Gnostics tried to broaden the list of supposed or
real apostolic writings. In the case of Marcion the opposite
was the case. He narrowed down the canon to just Luke

and ten epistles of Paul, all with a retouched text. The reason why he did not include the Pastorals, though they had already been written, was probably because he found them antagonistic to his doctrine. The reaction of the faithful, however, was the same. They had been used to hearing four Gospels read to them, together with letters of Peter and John. Restricting the canon meant the end of catholicity, that is to say, Christianity was only Pauline and Jewish-Christians were excluded, as were other Christian lineages. The campaigns *Adversus Marcionem*, therefore, were only logical.

The Montanist movement, or the 'Phrygians' as they were called, did not affect the canon directly, but claims of ecstatic prophecy by Montanus and Maximilla, who felt themselves in some way 'possessed' by God or Christ, threatened to add their prophetic utterances to the inspired Scriptures.

We find the first clear description of the place of readings from Scripture in the celebration of the Eucharist in Justin. In his First Apology (67) he says: 'And on the day called Sunday, all who live in cities or in the country gather together to one place and the memoirs of the apostles or the prophets are read, as long as time permits'.[6] The fact that the Scriptures were read to the people in a Eucharistic context reveals the real purpose of the canon. The Church identifies herself as *ecclesia* in the most solemn moment of her worship, and word and sacrament mutually interpret each other. The memory of the Emmaus episode may not be out of place in this context. It is the Risen Christ in person who explains the true sense of Scripture and breaks the bread. The canon, therefore, though always normative, is not an end in itself. The Church reads her own identity within the reciprocal interaction between word and sacrament.

Mutual exchange also occurs between word and reader: 'Those who are unspiritual do not receive the gifts of God's Spirit, for they are foolishness to them, and they are unable to understand them because they are spiritually discerned. Those who are spiritual discern all things, and they are not subject to no one else's scrutiny' (1Cor 2:14–15). Moses' veil which covers the true meaning of the Old Testament in 2 Cor 3:14–18 can also cover the New Testament if it is read with unspiritual eyes: 'Now the Lord is the Spirit, and where the Spirit of the Lord is, there is freedom. And all of us, with unveiled faces, seeing the glory of the Lord, as though reflected in a mirror, are transformed into the same image from one degree of glory to another; for this comes from the Lord, the Spirit'. This recalls the anointing in 1John 2:27–28 which endows the believer with the spirit of discernment.

The Scriptures were always seen as the word of God by both Jews and Christians. But when did the writings contained in the New Testament begin to be considered as Scripture on a par with those of the Old Testament? We have already found a hint in 2Pt 3:16 where the author equates Paul's letters with 'the other Scriptures'. The Seer of Revelation is also conscious of transmitting God's word with authority, as shown by the seven letters to the Churches in chapters 2 and 3. Justin speaks of the prophets and the memoirs of the apostles in one breath, but it was only in the second half of the second century that the writings obtained scriptural status.

The best witnesses to the canon, however, are the deacons and readers who refused to hand over the Scriptures during the great persecutions. They even tried to trick the collectors by delivering apocrypha or other books, but the collectors were well trained to distinguish which books were held sacred by the Christians and proceeded to arrest their deceivers.

If the New Testament was held to be Scripture by Christians, this means that its text was taken to be the word of God like the Old Testament itself, that is to say, it was inspired.

The NT canon, therefore, was not imposed by Popes, bishops or emperors. It emerged among many other writings that claimed to be Christian merely because the Churches mirrored, and defined themselves by, these ancient books, which, indeed, were the foundations of their faith. In the last resort, apostolicity, universal public reading and agreement with the rule of faith are the essential criteria.

Notes

1. W. R. Farmer and D. M. Farkasfalvy, *The Formation of the New Testament Canon* (New York, 1983), pp. 110–117.
2. Cf. *The Letter of James to Peter*, I,3 and *Homilies*, II, 17; XI,5.
3. See E. E. Urbach, *The Sages, their Concepts and Beliefs* (Jerusalem, 1979), pp. 543f.
4. B. Metzger, *The Canon of the New Testament* (Oxford, 1987), p. 55.
5. See Eusebius' distinction in *Historia Ecclesiastica*, III, xxv, 1–7.
6. Whether Justin's two Apologies were separate writings or one divided into two is under discussion. See C. H. Munier, *Sources Chrétiennes* 507 (Paris, 2006) who opines that there was actually one Apology transmitted in two parts.

5 ALTERNATIVE CHRISTIANITIES?

A NUMBER OF PATRISTIC scholars allege that today's Christianity, the heir of so-called 'Mainstream Christianity', the Great Church of the first three centuries, is only one of many other legitimate forms of Christianity. They did not survive because they were stamped out by the Church. Is this a proper interpretation of history? There is no easy answer to this question. The infinite number of permutations and combinations of scholarly opinion regarding the definition of Christianity, and problems arising from recent studies on Jewish Christianity and Gnosticism, liken any definite answer to a construction built on quicksand. We can only try to expound some arguments to help the reader to come to some sort of conclusion on this issue.

What is *a* Christianity? Which religion can rightly claim to be Christian?[1] It would be easy to give an *a priori* definition to legitimise one's conclusion, but that would only be a vicious circle. An empirical approach, as far as this is feasible, is certainly more fruitful.

Christianity has its roots in the historical person of Jesus of Nazareth, called the Christ. A simple acknowledgment of Jesus would not be sufficient. The Quran speaks well of Jesus and Mary but that does not make it Christian. The real question is what *Christ* means. Does it entail Sonship and the Incarnation, or can the epithet be interpreted in some other way?

We said earlier that in the first century of its existence Christianity had various forms: there were Pauline, Johan-

nine, Petrine and Jewish Christians, each with their own
theology, sometimes conflicting, but not contradictory, so
much so that they later came together in one canon of
mainstream Christianity—the Great Church. There were
also Jewish-Christians, namely Jews who believed in Jesus
as the Christ, the Son of God. Some of them rejected this
latter title because they could not reconcile it with their
monotheism. However, they did retain their title as 'Christian', but among them the Ebionites[2] believed that the
Christ descended on Jesus at his baptism, thus separating
the two entities. All these currents professed Christ as the
Saviour; his person was central and faith in him was the
core of their religion. This is what distinguished them from
pure Judaism and pagan religions.

Early in the second century, Gnostic movements
emerged.[3] In some of them we find the terms 'Christ',
'saviour', 'Jesus', 'son', 'son of man', '*ekklesia*', logos, '*pistis*',
as we do in the Gospels. Others do not mention Christ at
all. They were just simple theosophies of the Hellenistic
world. The central question now is: did the above terms
have the same meaning as those used by earlier Christian
believers? Was Christ central in their religion or was he
only a peripheral figure implanted in a foreign system
whose core differed substantially from Christianity, which
was marked out by its faith in Christ? We find this happen-
ing in some eclectic sects and theosophies of our own times.
Can they be called Christian, a genuine alternative to
contemporary mainstream Christianity from which the
Church was born, or are they just alternative religions?

Nicola Denzey Lewis states the question very well in her
recent book *Introduction to "Gnosticism": Ancient Voices,
Christian Worlds.*[4] She traces various opinions from Hans
Jonas, through the 1966 Messina Conference, Michael
Williams and Karin King to the so-called Yale School. The

table she presents on p. 18 in which Nag Hammadi documents can be classified as Gnostic, attests to the variety of
opinions among modern scholars about what qualifies a
book as Gnostic or not. The Messina distinction between
Gnosis and Gnosticism may facilitate the question but it
does not solve the problem. I myself find it difficult to shake
off Hans Jonas' thesis that Gnosticism is essentially a
philosophical existential problem in Middle Platonism that
tackles the problem of evil, borrowing ideas from Judaism,
Christianity, mythology and magic.[5]

It is obvious that here we cannot enter the inextricable
labyrinth of Gnostic thought. The definition of Gnosticism
itself is at stake. Is it a term imposed by modern scholars
on the various groups of the second and third centuries
who relied on knowledge—*gnosis*—for their salvation, or
did it arise from their self-awareness? Do they have any
common denominator that allows us to perceive their
similarities to, and differences from, mainstream Christian
communities? The problem is as old as Irenaeus. In his
time, various Gnostics approached traditional Christians
to attract them to their meetings. They spoke a language
that was so similar to that heard in church that the hearers
thought there would be no harm in giving them a chance
if this led to higher knowledge. It may be important to note
that the Gnostics approached Christians and not pagans
to attract proselytes. Similar terminology can have differing meanings, however. The words 'liberty' and 'democracy' are used to define the political status of the USA,
China, Russia and Africa but when interpreted within the
context of the political ideology of each nation they end
up by having completely opposite meanings.

The Gnostics also took over the literary genres of the
books read by the Christians: gospels, Acts, letters and the

apocalypse. This means that the NT canon was already asserting itself and provided a model for later writings.

Irenaeus tried to decode their language within its real context and was compelled to alert Victor, the Bishop of Rome, about the extensive spread of Gnosticism in that city. By means of a detailed study of the literature on which he could lay his hands, he pointed out the essential differences between Christian and Gnostic theology. Modern scholars, with numerous original Gnostic documents to hand, can judge whether Irenaeus and other Fathers were right or not.

Ambiguous terminology, however, may not be ambiguous at all but genuinely Christian, and this leads us to two other thorny problems: a grading of our documents according to their degree of Christian content, on the one hand, and the origins of Gnosticism, on the other. Given the vast literature on the subject, I will confine myself here to stating the question and expressing a cautious opinion.

There are Christian books with a touch of Gnosticism like, perhaps, *the Gospel of Thomas*. I use the word 'Christian' to denote mainstream Christianity so as not to prejudge the issue of possible alternative Christianities. At the opposite extreme we find purely Gnostic documents, with no Christian features at all. In between are works of various levels of assimilation of Christianity, presenting a heavenly Christ as saviour, dialogues of the risen Jesus with his disciples, and mention of the death of Jesus and his relationship with the Christ. Most of the Gnostic books are full of Jewish names borrowed from fringe Jewish movements of the inter-testamental period. The core of Gnostic speculation, however, is the prevailing Middle Platonism of the day. Many categories are those of the *Hermetica*. One can say that the Gospel and Letters of John also speak a similar language,[6] but whereas John uses this language to illustrate his faith in Jesus, the Gnostic writings introduce the figure of Christ to lend a touch of Christianity to Hellenistic speculation and render it more palatable to simple believers.

This leads to the other question of the origins of Gnosticism, at which we can only hint.[7] The ample references to the Old Testament and Judaism, as well as its Hellenistic concepts, point to the probability of contacts between fringe Jewish groups with contemporary Hellenistic thought. We find this in Philo as well, but whereas the Alexandrian scholar wanted to present the Torah as a valid philosophy amongst others of the time, other Jews got carried away by esoteric eclectic theosophies, which, in the first half of the second century, gave birth to Gnostic groups that absorbed Christian ideas.[8]

The existence of Gnostic documents that contain no Christian doctrines poses the problem of whether they represent original Gnostic thought, to which Christian elements were added, or, as some scholars hold, the Christian elements were stripped off during the fourth or fifth century when Gnosticism had been banned by the Church. A classic case is the synoptic reading of the purely Gnostic *Eugnostos* and the 'Christian' *Sophia Jesu Christi.* They have many passages in common, and the problem reminds us of the discussion on the priority of Mark over Matthew which is adhered to by the vast majority of NT scholars. In other words, is Gnosticism a valid alternative to mainstream Christianity, a Christian heresy, a parasitic plant growing around the Church, or is it an autonomous non-Christian religion?[9]

At this point it is necessary to understand what we mean by 'heresy' as a technical term. The Greek *hairesis* can indicate a sect, a set of differing opinions. In Christian parlance, however, it means the outright persevering denial of a fundamental tenet of Christianity, with a possible schism. It is different from simple error which can be discussed and corrected. Arianism and Nestorianism were considered heresies, but they did not cease to be Christian— they were unorthodox Christian, but Christian all the same, because the central figure of their faith was Christ.

Had Gnosticism been a single, consistent system one could attempt an answer to the questions posed above, but as there were, as Irenaeus put it, as many Gnosticisms as there were Gnostics,[10] only a cursory reply is possible. We said above that the spectrum of Gnostic documents ranges from Christian ones with a touch of Gnosticism, through Gnostic ones soaked in Christian language, to completely non-Christian texts. The motivation they seem to have in common is *gnosis,* knowledge. But knowledge of what? They would have answered: the insight of some chosen ones of a divine self-identity of which people were unaware because of their existential slumber. They had to be woken up and, by means of a revelation, or by a revealer belonging to the pleromatic realm, made conscious of their true selves, so that this very self could be saved and returned to its nature. The revealer is sometimes Christ, a heavenly aeon who comes to impart this saving knowl- edge. The Valentinians spoke about *spiritual* persons, i.e. themselves as true Gnostics, assuredly saved; *psychics,* slumbering Christians who had to be enlightened; and *hylics,* material people for whom there was no salvation— the pagans.[11] It would be ironically paradoxical if the initiators of Gnosticism were themselves pagans.

Such a doctrine, however, had to be placed within a cosmogony. How did this fragment of spirit fall into this world and embed itself in matter, which was seen negatively in Platonic thought? If we believe in one good Creator how do we explain the existence of evil in the world? Gnostic systems try to answer this question each in their own way. What many had in common was that if there was an 'original sin', this occurred in the heavenly spheres, not among humans. While biblical tradition, therefore, tried to underline human responsibility for the presence of evil and appealed to faith and conversion for salvation from evil, Gnostics tended to de-responsibilise man and offered only self-knowledge as a means of salvation.

The controversial point between Christians and Gnostics was evidently Genesis 1–3. These chapters speak of one creator God who created a 'good, very good, world' and how the very first humans introduced chaos into it by their disobedience. The table of parallels of three Nag Hammadi documents, *Hypostasis of the Archons, Apocryphon of John* and *On the Origin of the World* in Nicola Lewes' book cited above,[12] very clearly sets out the differences between Jewish, Christian and Gnostic interpretations of the three chapters that open the Bible. The Gnostic hermeneutic is not an adaptation, correction or denial of Rabbinic or Patristic interpretations; it turns the obvious meaning of the scriptural texts inside out and upside down. There can be no dialogue or compromise between the two explanations. The Archon, angels or demiurge who made the world are the villains of the narrative. It is only the wisdom of some revealer, sometimes the Serpent, who can open the eyes of humans to look beyond the creator into the heavenly spheres in order to acknowledge their true substance. This seems to me to be no simple Christian heresy but an outright denial of Jewish and Christian core faith and the counter-proposition of a completely different theosophy. One can certainly subscribe to it, but not in the name of Christianity, whether it includes a Christ or not.

Anyone belonging to the school of Valentinus would have resented such an assertion, and rightly so, because the post-Valentinians developed an elaborate Gnostic Christology that was scarcely distinguishable from other second-century mainstream Christologies.[13] The heavenly Christ gathers within himself the aeons of the Valentinian pleroma, transforming them into attributes. He descended through all the spheres, collecting in himself all their natures, even a bodily nature, which was born of the Virgin Mary. Jesus' body, however, was psychic or spiritual, according to the western or eastern schools, but the heavenly Christ could not mix himself with a hylic, material body, as the body of Jesus was. The purpose of this 'incarnation' was the enlightenment of the chosen ones. Jesus died in reality, but this was not the case of the heavenly body of Christ. Hence we cannot talk of the redemptive death of one person. Moreover, to them the resurrection of the body, in a Platonic context, was absurd.

This intricate doctrine about the true nature of Christ posed real problems that took centuries to be resolved by the Church in its controversies with Arius, Apollinaris, Nestorius and Eutiches. In the second century, an ordinary Christian might have seen nothing wrong, though a little strange, in the Valentinian summary. A more learned one would have excluded it as a Docetic heresy. In truth, studied only in itself, this Christological construct was a Christian heresy, similar to Apollinaris' teaching about Christ being composed of a divine soul and a human body, stumbling against the maxim *quod non assumptum non redemptum*. But when inserted into the broader context of Gnostic thought it was more of a foreign body inserted into an alien Hellenistic edifice. Gnosis brought by a heavenly being called Christ, detached from a real human body, is not faith in Jesus *the* Christ, Son of God and Son of Man.

Gnostic theses	Mainstream Christianity
Creation by demiurge	One God creator
Matter evil	Creation good, very good
Fall in heavenly spheres	Fall in mankind
Revealer alerts man to true being	Christ reveals Father
Revealer sometimes called Christ	Revealer Jesus Christ
Salvation reconstruction of pleroma	Cosmic salvation
Body of Jesus docetic	Jesus had a material body
The Christ did not die on the cross	Jesus the Christ did die
Dialogue of the risen Christ with disciples	Jesus' teaching on earth
Spirit returns to pleroma	Resurrection of mankind
Humans grouped in three classes	No distinction
Serpent warns against creator	Serpent symbol of evil
Judas positive figure	Judas traitor
Gnostics proselytise Christians	Christians preach to all
Conversion awakening from sleep	Moral conversion
No resurrection of the flesh	Resurrection of the body
Salvation through knowledge	Salvation through faith
Figure of Christ secondary	Jesus Christ central

I am quite aware that my opinion on the nature and origin of Gnosticism as a parasitic plant entwined round the main trunk of Christianity is not subscribed to by everyone. Major scholars like Barbara Aland, Simone Pétrement and Manlio Simonetti hold that it is of Christian origin, soaked in Hellenistic speculation, and hence a Christian heresy. The preceding comparative table of the main doctrines of each religion will let the reader decide for himself. The Gnostic recurring theses are of course gathered from various systems in patristic and Nag Hammadi documents as no one document contains them all. The same holds good for Christian doctrines, contained in the various NT writings and the Rule of Faith. What unites the two is the theme of the salvation of humans in Christianity, of both the divine and the human in Gnosticism.

It seems to me that the contrasting beliefs of Christianity and Gnosticism are so profound that the latter can hardly be called an alternative Christianity. It is, rather, an alternative Hellenistic religion that absorbed and re-ordered Christian elements. The same *tesserae* of a mosaic can be rearranged to form another image.[14]

Notes

1. In this chapter we deal mainly with Gnosticism as this seems to be the major concern of the controversy after the discovery of the Nag Hammadi documents. But one wonders what shape the discussion would take if it were to be extended to all the sects and doctrines listed in Epiphanius' *Panarion* or in Augustine's *De haeresibus*. For a full bibliography on these texts from 1948–2006 see D. Scholer's three volumes published by Brill, Leiden, 2007.
2. Epiphanius attributes the foundation of the Ebionites to a certain Ebion. *Ebion*, however only means 'poor' in Hebrew, hence 'the Poor'. In the *Panarion*, 30–33 he gives a rather disparaging description of them but some traits coincide with what we can deduce about them from the Clementine Letters.

3. The majority of scholars today no longer speak about pre-Christian Gnosticism as had been done from Reitzenstien to Bultmann, but limit the term to the Gnostic groups that took shape in the first quarter of the second century. See Edwin Yamauchi, *Pre-Christian Gnosticism: A Survey of the Proposed Evidence* (London, 1973).
4. See N. Denzey Lewis, *Introduction to "Gnosticism": Ancient Voices, Christian Worlds* (Oxford, 2013), pp. 16–20.
5. H. Jonas, *The Gnostic Religion: The Message of the Alien God and the Beginnings of Christianity* (Boston, 1967[2]).
6. C. H. Dodd had already approached the question in *The Interpretation of the Fourth Gospel* (Cambridge, 1954), pp. 97–114.
7. Filoramo's excellent survey comes very near to a solution in G. Filoramo, *L'attesa della fine: Storia della gnosi.* (Rome, 1983).
8. Cf. H. A. Wolfson, *Philo: Foundations of Religious Philosophy in Judaism, Christianity and Islam* (Harvard, 1962), vol. I, pp. 3–86.
9. P. Grech, 'La gnosi: Un'eresia Cristiana?', *Augustinianum*, XXXV (1995), 587–596. But cf. M. Simonetti, *Testi gnostici in lingua greca e latina* (Milan, 2005), who in his introduction is of the opinion that Gnosticism is a Christian heresy, as are Petrement and B. Aland, in opposition to Filoramo.
10. St Irenaeus, *Adversus haereses*, I, 11 and 12.
11. *Ibid.*, I,1,5.
12. N. D. Lewis, *Introduction to "Gnosticism": Ancient Voices, Christian Worlds* (Oxford, 2013), pp. 273–278.
13. St Irenaeus, *Adversus haereses*, I,21.
14. To understand the true meaning of Gnostic terms that resemble the Christian ones cf. A. P. Smith, *A Dictionary of Gnosticism* (Wheaton, 2009).

6 DOCTRINAL DEVELOPMENT WITHIN THE CHURCH

W E BEGAN CHAPTER 3 with a long quotation from Vincent of Lerins. It is to this author that we must now return. It is he who, about the end of the fifth century, looked back on the growth of Christian belief from the apostolic period to his own times and elaborated a thesis to explain how the faith of the Church could develop while maintaining its original identity. The *Commonitorium* was taken up again in the nineteenth century by John Henry Newman whose book *An Essay on the Development of Christian Doctrine* is still a classic. In this chapter we shall turn to these two works, limiting our argument on the development of Christian doctrine to the patristic period.

The Bible is full of examples of the growth of revelation in the history of Israel and during the New Testament period. The monolatry of the Patriarchs became the monotheism of the prophets. Prophetic oracles were constantly reinterpreted to convey new meanings to subsequent generations. Wisdom literature imported Hellenistic thought to express Israel's faith. But within the books of the New Testament canon examples of development are also not lacking.[1] Certain terms, like 'Kingdom of God', 'Son of Man' and 'Son of God', which occur so frequently in the Synoptics, acquire different meanings in Paul and John. There are two points of view about the relationship of faith and good works in James and Paul. John goes his own way in interpreting the person of Christ

with the use of the term *Logos*. Luke anchors the Church
in history and underlines the fact that political, social and
religious events intertwine to contribute towards a development of Christian self-understanding, under the guid-
ance of the Spirit. The apostolic Church left many
unanswered questions.

The problems posed in the second century by Gnostics,
Docetists, Jews and Jewish Christians compel Justin,
Ignatius and Irenaeus to trace more clearly the boundaries
of self-identity. We witness the change from collective
leadership in the Churches to mono-episcopacy. The
Pastoral Letters attest to an embryonic 'canon law' that
aimed at a better structuring of the communities while
prophecy began to fade or to create problems. Moreover,
notwithstanding the convergence of the fundamental
tenets of Christianity as defined in Irenaeus' Rule of Faith,
each one of the various Churches grew within the heritage
of its founder. These local problems varied with the
growth of the Church, in which one province could enjoy
peace while another suffered persecution; one could be
blessed with excellent leadership while another was beset
by internal scandals. Yet, on the whole, the Church grew
in faith and deepened her theological reflection. It would
be superfluous to call to mind the transformation brought
about by the rise of Arianism and Constance's edict.

It is these problems that Vincent of Lerins set himself
to resolve in his *Commonitorium* when reviewing the
diversity of theological formulations down the centuries
that separated him from the Apostolic Church. Had
doctrine changed? Had it evolved or had it suffered
corruption, so that it could no longer claim to be apostolic?
What actually is orthodoxy and what is heresy? His treatise
gives clear answers to these questions, too clear perhaps,

as the modern reader is tempted to point to sundry holes in his arguments.

Vincent explains the word 'Catholic' in its etymological meaning of universality.[2] To be truly Catholic one must believe what has always been the Church's faith, what has been believed everywhere and by everyone. Antiquity takes us back to the apostolic period; universality prevents us from limiting faith to one or two provinces; one must understand what the whole Church professes.[3] 'By everyone' means by all bishops and doctors, especially when they express themselves at the general councils.

Vincent blames the Arians for all the disorders at and around Nicaea.[4] They presented a new doctrine by denying the *homoousios*, which only rendered explicit what had always been believed by the Church. It is well known that many pre-Nicene fathers were subordinationists though they acknowledged Jesus' divinity, and that after the definition the bishops who accepted the Council's decision were, for a time, in a minority.

The Lerinian appeals to St Paul to establish his doctrine, who exhorts the Romans to keep away from those who cause dissent and create scandals (Rom 16:17–18), and anathemises even an angel of God who dares to contradict his teaching (Gal 1:6–8; 5:16).[5] Vincent's favourite texts, however, are drawn from the Pastorals, particularly 1 Tim 1:19; 5:12–13: 6:4–5; 2 Tim 2:16–18; 3:6–9; and Tit 1:10–11. But his main emphasis is on 1 Tim 6:20–21, where the Apostle exhorts Timothy to guard closely the deposit of faith and keep away from dissenters. Vincent stresses the fact that Paul's warnings are limited neither to the Galatians nor to the Timothies of his time: they pertain to every subsequent period in the Church's history. Bishops and doctors should identify themselves with Timothy. They should also keep in mind Jesus' parables about the wheat and tares growing together (Mt 13:24–30) and the talents entrusted to the servants in Mt 25:15.

The monk of Lerins cites Pope Stephen's answer to Cyprian on the rebaptism of Christians who had offered sacrifices to idols: *Nihil innovetur nisi quod traditum est*,[6] and Ambrose' praise of those martyrs who had given their lives for the faith of their fathers.

'But why does God permit heresies?'[7] Vincent asks. He finds his answer in Deut 13:1–3 where Moses warns against false prophets who open the doors to idolatry. God permits this to refine the steadfastness in faith of His people. Paul gives the same answer in 1Cor 11:19. Such is Vincent's warning to those who are drawn to the teaching of Arius, Nestorius, Photinus and Apollinaris.[8] He is even unhappy with Origen and Tertullian who, in spite of their great merits and learning, deviated at some points from right doctrine. Heretics are versed in Scripture, but even Satan can cite Scripture for his purpose![9]

If we always repeat the same teaching, are we not in danger of stagnation?[10] Can there be no progress in dogma? This is Vincent's main concern and his answer to that question is his main contribution to theology. No, he says, Catholic doctrine is not static; it evolves, it grows and develops, but without ever modifying or corrupting what had been said earlier. The faith grows according to the intelligence, knowledge and wisdom of individuals, of the community, of persons and of the whole Church according to the age and century, provided this takes place in line with the peculiar nature of each dogma, with the same meaning and the same interpretation. Vincent makes use of two analogies: the organic growth of the human body and the seed that develops into a plant. Both manifest an essential transformation but maintain their original identity. Roses cannot develop into thorns. This is the way dogma grows.[11] By cultivating what was planted by the Fathers in the field of the Church, we can be sure that the seeds will flourish and bear fruit. If we ever permit corruption even in one single doctrine we will open the door to similar modifications in other dogmas. The Church has always encouraged this development of doctrines until they reached their maturity in the general councils, were summarised into formulas and expressed in more meaningful terms to each generation.

It is only the *regula fidei* that requires the universal consent of those Fathers who led a holy life, were endowed with true wisdom and expressed what had been always held by their predecessors.[12] It is to these Fathers that the bishops united in council appeal to assert authentic doctrine, as the recent Council of Ephesus had shown.

Vincent's last chapter pays tribute to the Apostolic See in Rome and recalls Popes Stephen, Celestine and Sixtus who did their utmost to uphold Church tradition against heretical novelties.[13]

Vincent's subject, with some minor intermediate steps, was taken up by John Henry Newman fourteen centuries later, first in his *University Sermons* and later in *An Essay on the Development of Christian Doctrine*[14] which was written while he was still an Anglican and thoroughly revised in 1878 after he had been received into the Roman Catholic Church. The book can only be summarised by transcribing its 'Contents'. Newman's notions are not easy to grasp at first reading. In what follows I can only present an outline, with the hope that it is not a caricature.

Newman had been convinced that the Anglican Church was the true Catholic Church because it preserved the core of Apostolic preaching, from which the Roman Church had deviated by adding new dogmas and the Protestants had deviated by neglecting this tradition. Little by little he gave way to the concern that the 'deviations' of the Romans were not deviations at all, but a doctrinal development in continuity with what had characterised the growth of Christian belief down the centuries. His concern became a conviction.

Newman accepts with caution Vincent's analogy of the organic growth of an individual from birth to manhood, but he does not develop it.[15] His own keynote is the development of a self-standing idea. It may be implicit, but it unfolds not by means of explanation but through reflection.[16] The original intuition gives rise to further doctrines, even to new dogmas. There is an implicit and an explicit reason: an inward idea of divine truth defines and delineates itself by the activity of our reflective powers. This process is not essential, however; an uneducated person might not develop his intuitions at all, and a seminal idea may remain buried for centuries until it calls to come out in all its clarity. It does not do this by logical explication but by the eruption of its dynamic possibilities. An idea has many facets, and each facet is endowed with the possibility of development. Indeed, a 'seminal idea' contains also a 'principle' to which it is subject and which indicates the right path of its development.

Newman posits seven 'notes', or criteria, of genuine growth, to each of which he dedicates a chapter of explanation.[17] These are: 1. genuine development of an idea and preservation of its type; 2. continuity of its principle; 3. its power of assimilation; 4. its logical sequence; 5. anticipation of its future; 6. conservative action upon its past; and 7. its chronic vigour. These are not infallible criteria but a 'hypothesis to account for a difficulty'. They do point, however, to genuine growth if taken cumulatively, to a development along the lines of the backbone principle. They are not a deviation or a corruption of the original idea. Power of assimilation means being open to dialogue, with one eye on the past and the other on the future within a logical process. Although external factors may cause or occasion some steps forward, its growth is due to its native vigour and internal dynamism.

Newman's theory of the developing idea is a generic one. It can be applied in any area, to 'democracy', for example. It is not specifically theological. In the theological field, the nuclear idea with the many facets that yearn to develop is the apostolic deposit, as found in Scripture and in the Rule of Faith. In this case, however, together with the idea's internal dynamism, the prevailing power is that of the Holy Spirit.[18] Our author attributes the emergence of the canon of Scripture, original sin, infant baptism, communion under one kind, the *homoousios*, the Incarnation, the dignity of the Mother of God and papal supremacy itself to this innate potential. There is a real advance in the Church's teaching; it is not merely logical deduction or explanation. New dogmas are produced that maintain the identical principle in spite of the newness of the ideas. Newness is not novelty. It is not a deviation, much less corruption, but a rendering explicit of the possibilities of the various facets of the original idea. The apostles might not have foreseen these further developments but had they known them they would have expressed their surprise to admit that they are but the logical consequence of the principles they laid down once and forever. We are speaking here of a continuing revelation, not the creation of novel truths but the uncovering of what lay hidden in the old ones. This may remind us of Heidegger's description of truth as the unveiling of being. It is the growth of 'the inward idea of divine truth' subjected to human reflection. Just as an Aristotelian scholar will tell you what Aristotle would have said on some topic or other, so the Popes and the councils read the apostles' minds on the doctrinal problems of their day.

Vincent of Lerins' *Commonitorium* certainly set the stage for the definition of doctrinal development in the Second Vatican Council (*Dei Verbum*, 8), but Newman carried the day in the Council's discussions.

Christian development of thought can fall into the category of the development of philosophical ideas, or of historical progress, if we apply Newman's theory of a developing idea. What differentiates the two categories is the role within the Church of the Holy Spirit who speaks through liturgical prayer, through the ordinary Magisterium, through the *sensus fidelium*, through historical circumstances and through social change.

Gradual illumination is not new revelation. Perhaps we can understand this better if we imagine the curtain of a theatre opening on a dark stage. We can distinguish a few figures who, we sense, are the actors, as well as some props. With the gradual turning up of the stage lights the persons and objects become clearer. Then we recognise the faces and, lastly, we hear them speak. Our engagement with the play is now complete. It is not the realities that have changed but our understanding of them.

It is heresies that contributed most to the emergence of orthodoxy. A theologian publishes a book proposing some doctrine or other. The general readership perceives that something in that book 'does not fit the pattern'. It disturbs the sense of faith of ordinary Christians. Then a theologian or other will indicate the reasons for this shock. A discussion among other theologians begins and gradually they begin to distinguish the disturbing elements from what is acceptable. If the new teaching becomes widely threatening then a synod or a council is necessary to define the truth of the matter, expressed perhaps in new contemporary terms but retaining its roots in tradition. This was what the doctrines rejected by Nicaea, Ephesus and Chalcedon occasioned. Without these errors we would have been poorer. Of course there will be anathemas that appear to suppress alternative faiths but in reality they underline the continuity of new articles of faith with 'what was from the beginning'. Anathemas concern all that threatens to disfigure the person or the saving mission of Christ.

Notes

1. Cf. P. Grech, 'The Beginnings of Christian Theology' in A. di Berardino and B. Studer (eds.), *History of Theology: The Patristic Period* (Minnesota, 1997), vol. I, pp. 17–81.
2. St Vincent of Lerins, *Commonitorium*, 2.
3. *Ibid.*, 4.
4. *Ibid.*, 4.
5. *Ibid.*, 8.
6. *Ibid.*, 6.
7. *Ibid.*, 10.
8. *Ibid.*, 18.
9. *Ibid.*, 26.
10. *Ibid.*, 23.
11. *Ibid.*, 23.
12. *Ibid.*, 27.
13. *Ibid.*, 32.
14. J. H. Newman, *An Essay on the Development of Christian Doctrine*. Reprint 1989 of the sixth edition (1868), Notre Dame, Indiana, Preface by Ian Ker.
15. *Ibid.*, p. 172.
16. *Ibid.*, pp. 55ff.
17. *Ibid.*, pp. 169–206.
18. *Ibid.*, pp. 122–168.

7 EMPERORS, POPES AND COUNCILS

T HAT OUR CREEDAL confessions on the Trinity and the Incarnation emerged from a century of theological discussions, political intrusions, social conflicts and papal input is nothing less than miraculous. Preaching, didactic treatises and disciplinary provisions usually follow Church tradition in times of peace. However, when this peace is disturbed by someone who proposes strange doctrines that do not fit into the common pattern, a reaction is bound to set in. The debates concerning the date of Easter, Adoptiomism, dynamic or modalistic Monarchianism, and Sabellianism in the latter half of the third century prepared the way for the Arian crisis. This began as an internal Christian controversy, but, with the accession of Constantine, it soon became a political issue. Mutual excommunications occurred among bishops, appeals to the Roman Church, physical acts of violence and insubordination to conciliar decrees. Old animosities between East and West were enhanced by the split of the Empire and these were not helped by the submission of the Eastern Churches to political power and by the lack of a clear ecclesiology. Rome was certainly considered the source and symbol of unity as the Chair of Peter but it was the Council of Chalcedon that finally clarified the hierarchy of the apostolic Churches.[1]

This chapter is neither about the primacy of Peter or the Pope nor about the latter's infallibility. We will begin with an outline of the standing of Rome in order to have a better understanding of the later interplay between councils and politics, as well as between differences in ecclesiological views in the East and in the West.

Christianity arrived in Rome prior to the arrival of Peter and Paul, as the Letter to the Romans shows (cf. Acts 28:14–15). The preaching of these two apostles to Jews and gentiles, and especially their martyrdom, however, endowed that Church with a distinctive authority. The other Churches honoured the See of Peter, as it came to be called, and often appealed to its judgment on matters or discipline and doctrine. On the other hand, this Church from the very beginning was conscious of a certain prerogative that enabled it to intervene and interact with other Churches by means of pronouncements, dialogue and controversy.[2]

At its birth, the Roman community was mainly composed of Jewish Christians who had difficulties regarding common meals with gentile converts (cf. Rom 12–13). The subject of the arrival of the monoepiscopate in the city, an institution that was already widespread in Asia Minor, is still uncertain. Ignatius, contrary to his usual practice, does not mention the name of the bishop in his letter to the Romans. On the other hand Irenaeus,[3] Hegessippus[4] and others have left us lists of Roman bishops up to their own time, always starting with Peter and his immediate successors: Linus, Anacletus, Clement, etc., who might have presided over a college of presbyters. The role and title of bishop as we find them in the Ignatian letters fall within the category of developing faith as described in the preceding chapter.

Clement's First Letter to the Corinthians is the oldest example of Rome's intervention outside its own territory. It is an epistle which has the intent of offering a brotherly correction to a sister Church with internal difficulties over the deposition of certain presbyters. Its tone is authoritative and the author is conscious of writing with the illumination of the Holy Spirit.[5] Walter Bauer maintained that orthodoxy was imposed by Rome by acting on the Church of Corinth as a bridge to the East, often by means of material help. This opinion has not received much support. Actually Rome was much closer to Alexandria as far as the Eastern Churches were concerned.

Next in line as a witness to Rome as a criterion of orthodoxy is Irenaeus whose well known text in *Adversus haereses* 3,3,2 has already been quoted in chapter 3. We need to quote part of it again in order to subject it to further analysis:

> For with this church, [i.e. the Church of Rome founded by the apostles Peter and Paul, which preserves the apostolic tradition] because of its superior origin, all churches must agree, that is, all the faithful in the whole world; it is in her that all the faithful everywhere have maintained the apostolic tradition.

Unfortunately we do not have the Greek original of this text, only its Latin translation which reads:

> *Ad hanc enim ecclesiam, propter po(ten)tiorem principalitatem, necesse est omnem convenire ecclesiam, hoc est, eos qui sunt undique fideles, in qua semper ab his, qui sunt undique [or: qui praesunt ecclesiis] conservata est ea quae est ab apostolis traditio.*

The translation presents some problems and some scholars have tried to retranslate it into its original language with arguable success. The shorter reading *potiorem* would be preferable to *potentioritatem principalitatem* but does not alter the meaning substantially. *Principalitas* can be understood in the sense of superiority, but in the context the temporal meaning 'because of its ancient origin' gives a better rendering, especially if the Greek was *arché*, as some commentators surmise. The main difficulty is the role of the faithful in preserving Rome's prerogative. The obvious sense it that their confluence in the city gives it universality.

Some authors translate *ab his* as 'for the sake of the faithful everywhere', which is a little overstretched. The main meaning of the entire text, however, is clearly that the Roman Church, because it was founded by Peter and Paul and aware of its antiquity, is a point of reference for all Christians as regards Christian truth. Nevertheless, it is worth noting that Irenaeus found it necessary to warn Pope Victor that Rome abounded with Gnostic sects.

Again, although Irenaeus[6] was certain about Rome's prerogative of preserving the traditions of Peter and Paul, he might have been less certain about some hurried disciplinary decisions of the Roman Bishop. He had to intervene personally on two occasions to soften the threat of imminent excommunication. Firstly, he asked Pope Victor to refrain from cutting off from Rome those Asian Churches that observed the quartordeciman tradition of celebrating Easter the day after the fourteenth of Nisan. Victor insisted that Easter must be celebrated on the following Sunday, as in Rome. The eastern bishops appealed to the most ancient apostolic traditions going back to John, Philip and Polycarp. Irenaeus, true to the etymology of his name, insisted on tolerance for the sake of peace among the Churches.

The second episode concerns the New Prophecy propagated by Montanus. The Roman Bishop Eleutherus threatened to cut him off but it was Irenaeus who carried a letter of petition to him from the imprisoned Christians of Lyon appealing to the Pope for a milder judgement. Later, according to the Montanist Tertullian, Praxeas the 'patripasian' convinced Callistus not to receive Montanus and thus he 'managed two pieces of the devil's business: he drove out prophecy and introduced heresy, he put to flight the Paraclete and crucified the Father'.[7]

These episodes reveal that, already in the second century, Rome was conscious of its authority, albeit open to dialogue with the other Churches. It was actually Pope Victor who excommunicated the Monarchian Theodotus. As far as Italy was concerned, Rome was certainly acknowledged as the mother of all the Churches in that country. This recognition was also shared by the West, including Africa, whose bishops and councils often appealed to Rome for advice and decisions as to doctrine.

Cyprian's dealings with Pope Stephen are a classic example of how this dialogue was carried on, albeit not without distress.[8] Around the middle of the third century Decius' persecution had produced many defections, either through sacrifice to the gods or through the acquisition of a *libellus*. When the persecution ceased many who had lapsed wanted to return to the Church. How were these penitents to be treated? Cyprian followed the general practice of admitting them to the ranks of the penitents. Thereby he was not only in agreement with Stephen, the Bishop of Rome, but he also paid him homage in spite of his belief in the equality of all bishops.

The situation became more critical when the question of rebaptism of those who had been baptised by heretics arose. Cyprian was well versed in Scripture but less so in theological tradition. He maintained, contrary to Roman and general custom, that since no one can give what he does not possess, a heretic could not communicate grace. This argument from reason contradicted the tradition of receiving these converts as penitents. Cyprian was backed by the African bishops and local councils. Their appeal to Rome only provoked Stephen's famous sentence: '*nihil innovetur nisi quod traditum est*'. This awkward Latin has the meaning of 'No novelties, just follow traditional custom'—the ancient custom of Rome and other

Churches. Neither Cyprian nor the Africans accepted this decision, which seemed unreasonable to them. We can say that this was Rome's first essential contribution to theological orthodoxy. The Africans lacked an adequate ecclesiology and knowledge of the working of a sacrament. The answer was provided later by Augustine whose well-known principle—whether it is Peter who baptises or Judas, it is Christ who baptises—gave rise to what we call today the sacramental *opus operatum*.[9]

We now come to the Arian crisis. The Church's faith in Father, Son and Holy Spirit is as old as Jesus' command to baptise in Mt 28:19 and the Trinitarian confessions in the New Testament letters. In the Johannine prologue the Logos was not only with God from the beginning but is God. Stephen addressed the Lord Jesus in Acts 7:59, and Pliny[10] observes that the Christians prayed to Jesus as to a God. But even among the earliest Fathers we discover a hint of subordination of the Son to the Father, a kind of 'second God'. Moreover, the Holy Spirit often fell into the OT category of the Power of God. Paul of Samosata stretched this subordination to the extreme and can be called the father of Arianism. He was condemned by synods of his own Church in Antioch.[11]

Arius accepted the monarchic insistence on the absolute oneness of God, but he also confessed the Logos as the creator of the world. He resolved the paradox by saying that the Logos was the first being created by the Father and by him subsequently everything was made. Hence his typical phrase: 'There was a time when he was not'. For such an assertion he could appeal to the Wisdom books of the Old Testament. Wisdom is there defined as God's first creature who assists him in his creation (Prov 8:22ss and compare Wis 7 with Hebr 1:2–4). It penetrates the whole universe and whoever follows it is sure to please

God. John's prologue and many of Jesus' sayings in the Fourth Gospel have wisdom as their background. With a shift in the *distinctio verborum* of the prologue, the Arians adapted it to their teaching.[12]

In spite of Paul of Samosata's deposition, Arianism spread like wildfire throughout the whole empire. Emperor Constantine, recently converted to Christianity, saw this division as a serious threat to the unity of his domains, and called for a council of bishops to decide the question. About 200 bishops met in Nicaea in 325 and at this council Athanasius played the main part. The council condemned Arius, defining that the Son was *homoousios* (consubstantial) with the Father. A creed was drawn up that crystallised the traditional rule of faith, but this did not settle the controversy at all. It went on for over half a century.[13] After the death of Constantine, Constans I ruled the West and Constantius II the East, and they and their followers sided with one party or the other. Eusebius of Nicomedia was the main adversary of Athanasius and the Nicaeans. His success was so great that there was a period when very few bishops upheld the *homoousios*. Some tried to compromise by changing the term to *homoiousios* (similar to the Father), which the Nicaeans could not accept. In 342 (343?) the bishops met again at Sardica (modern Sophia) to supplement Nicaea. They upheld Athanasius' doctrine. This is not seen as an ecumenical council but it was a suitable appendix to the former council. In all this turmoil what were the faithful to believe? It is actually they who carried the day: their inborn *sensus fidei* warned them against the pretentions of the Eusebian party. Theological discussions did not take place only among the bishops. Laymen debated the problems of faith among themselves even in the taverns. Through their perseverance in the traditional faith, Arianism fizzled out some decades later.

In 381, under Emperor Theodosius, a council was called at Constantinople to confirm the decisions of Nicaea which were held firmly by the West but still debated in the East.[14] Actually, no Western bishop was present. Unfortunately, we do not have the minutes of what took place there. The bishops confirmed the *homoousios* of the Nicene Creed, to which they added their faith in the divinity of the Holy Spirit, who proceeds from (and is not generated by) the Father. This was St. Basil's contribution in his later works. The confession of faith became known as the Nicene-Constantinopolitan Creed. From then on, the belief in one God, Father, consubstantial Son, and Holy Spirit prevailed in the whole Church.

One canon of this council, however, brought some confusion. The Bishop of Constantinople was declared to have the second rank of honour after the Bishop of Rome. The Easterners thus betrayed the ancient tradition of evaluating the dignity of a Church by means of its antiquity and apostolic origin: here they added a political criterion which is still a problem in the Orthodox Church.

However, there remained some Christological problems to be resolved. That Christ was Son of God and Son of Man was believed from the very beginning, but how did the realities expressed by these two titles coexist? Mary had been called *theotokos* from the second century onwards. She brought Jesus into the world, but how could she be the Mother of He who created her? Hence, Nestorius, following the suggestion of Theodore of Mopsuestia, opined that that there were two *prosopa* in Christ, two distinct realities, the divine and the human, whose characteristics were not to be confused. Mary could be called the Mother of Christ, *christotokos,* but not the Mother of God, *theotokos.* This was Antiochian thinking and somewhat Aristotelian. Cyril of Alexandria opposed Nestorius' teaching and appealed to Pope Celestine of Rome to pronounce a sentence against this heretic. Celestine assembled a synod of bishops in Rome and condemned Nestorius, leaving it to Cyril to put the sentence into effect. Nestorius appealed to Rome but to no effect and then to the Emperor who decided that the question should be decided by a council. Leaving aside the rather complicated history of the procedures of the Council of Ephesus in 431, and how it reached its decisions, the fact remains that the bishops defined the doctrine of *theotokos* at Ephesus in 431, citing Celestine's pristine decision, which was approved by the Emperor and by the Bishop of Rome. Christ was therefore one person, both God and man, and Mary, by giving birth to him, brought God into the world, in which sense she is His Mother.

This was bound to provoke a reaction. Euthyches so stressed the oneness of Christ that he came up with a mixture of divine and human natures in Christ's person. Euthyches thus brought to its final conclusion the doctrine of Apollinaris which had been formerly condemned by Rome and Alexandria, namely, that Christ had a human body and soul, but his spirit was divine. This would mean that Jesus was not entirely human. Monophisism, as Euthyches' doctrine was dubbed, was the main subject of discussion at the Council of Chalcedon which was held twenty years after Ephesus.

We will not enter here into the details of the Council of Chalcedon. But it is of the utmost importance because it contains, first of all, the fullest Catholic confession of faith about how Jesus Christ is to be conceived as God and man. Secondly, Rome and its Bishop Leo attained an acknowledgment of their full authority by both East and West. We may quote the Christological definition in full:

[The Council] opposes those who attempt to divide the mystery of the incarnation into two Sons. It excludes from the sacred assembly those who dare to declare subject to suffering the divinity of the Only Begotten. It withstands those who imagine a mixture or confusion of Christ's two natures (*physis*). It rejects those who fancy that the form of servant assumed by him among us is of a heavenly nature and foreign to us in essence (*ousis*). It condemns those who invent the myth of two natures of the Lord before the union and of one nature after the union.

Following therefore the holy Fathers, we unanimously teach to confess one and same Son, our Lord Jesus Christ, the same perfect in divinity and perfect in humanity, the same truly God and truly man, composed of rational soul and body, the same one in being (*homoousios*) with the Father as to the divinity and one in being *homoousios*) with us in the humanity, like unto us in all things but sin (Heb 4: 15) the same was begotten from the Father before the ages as to the divinity and in the later days for us and our salvation was born as to his humanity from Mary the virgin Mother of God.

We confess that one and the same Lord Jesus Christ, the only begotten Son, must be acknowledged in two natures, without confusion or change, without division or separation. The distinction between the natures was never abolished by the union but rather the character proper to each of the two natures was preserved as they came together in one person (*prosopon*) and one hypostasis. He is not split or divided into two persons but he is one and the same Only-begotten, God the Word, the Lord Jesus Christ, as formerly the prophets and later Jesus Christ Himself have told

us about him and as has been handed down to us
by the Symbol of the Fathers.

As these points have been determined by us with
all possible precision and care, the holy ecumenical
Council has ordained that no one may propose,
put into writing, devise, hold or teach to others any
other faith than this.[15]

This classic definition sums up the condemnation of Arius,
Nestorius, Apollinaris and Euthyches. It canonises the terms
ousia, prosopon and *homoousios.* It clarifies that there is one
person in Christ in two natures, completely human and
completely divine, neither mixed nor divided. Lastly, the
Council completes the Nicene-Constantinopolitan Creed.

It took Leo two years to approve the decisions of the
Council as requested by a synodal letter addressed to the
Pope at the end of the Council. The reason for the delay
was that it included the famous twenty-eighth canon. It did
acknowledge the authority of the Bishop of ancient Rome
and his right to approve the conciliar decisions. This canon,
however, also raised the Bishop of Constantinople almost
to the same rank. The canon had been formulated and
approved by a minority of bishops (perhaps 84 out of about
550) in the absence of the Roman legates. Leo refused to
accept this canon for the simple reason that it contradicted
the ancient tradition of ranking the Churches by their
apostolicity and antiquity. This was simply a political move.

The deference with which the Bishop of Rome was
addressed as the successor to the Blessed Peter also indicates that the Eastern bishops now accepted Rome's
primacy in deciding on matters of doctrine and that without
its approval the conciliar decisions would lack validity.

Leo did not usurp this power. He was only gathering
the fruits of a plant as old as Clement and Irenaeus, whose
seed was Christ's words to Peter in Mt 16:18.

It would be superfluous to continue with the aftermath of Chalcedon. The point of this chapter has been to show the factors in the development of the criteria of orthodoxy through storms and calm weather in the sense of doctrinal evolution as considered in the previous chapter.

Notes

1. See J. Lössl, *The Early Church: History and Memory* (London, 2010).
2. See M. Winter, *Saint Peter and the Popes* (London, 1960), a very balanced study from the Catholic point of view; and the excellent collection of documents on this matter in E. Giles, *Documents Illustrating Papal Authority* (London, 1952), with arguments pro and con.
3. St Irenaeus, *Adversus haereses*, 3,3,3.
4. In Eusebius, *Historia ecclesiastica*, 4,22.
5. Clement, *First Letter to the Corinthians*, 63,2.
6. Eusebius, *Historia ecclesiastica*, 5,23,1ff; 24,9–11.
7. Tertullian, *Adversus Praxean*, 130,1.
8. Cf. Giles, *Documents Illustrating Papal Authority*, pp. 49–66.
9. St Augustine, *Tractatus in Johannis Evangelium*, 5,18.
10. Pliny, *Epistula* X, 96.
11. As this synod is mentioned only by Hilarius some scholars doubt whether it ever took place. See H. C. Brenneke, 'Zum Fragen gegen Paul von Samosata', *Zeitschrift für die neutestamentliche Wissenschaft und die Kunde der älteren Kirche* 75 (1974), 270–290; P. de Navascués, *Pablo de Samosata y sus adversarios. Estudio histórico-teológico del cristianismo antioqueno en el siglo III*, *Studia Ephemeridis Augustinianum* 87 (Roma, 2004).
12. St Augustine, *De doctrina Christiana*, 3,2,3.
13. See J. Stevenson, *Creeds, Councils and Controversies: Documents Illustrating the History of the Church, A.D. 337–461* (London, 1989).
14. J. F. Kelly, *The Ecumenical Councils of the Catholic Church* (Minnesota, 2009), pp. 29–31.
15. Symbol of Chalcedon in DS 301–303.

8 LEX ORANDI

W HEN WE SPOKE about tradition we said that tradition and the rule of faith are two strings that intertwine. We now add a third—Christian prayer. The principle attributed to St. Prosper of Aquitaine—*ut legem orandi lex statuat credendi*—says that our prayers reflect our faith, and this obviously applies to any religion. We saw in chapter 3 that the Fathers often appealed to the rule of prayer to establish the orthodoxy of their theological statements. In this chapter we intend to illustrate this practice by means of some examples from Christian liturgy. This is far from being a history of Christian prayer; its purpose is only to cite some examples to show how the rule of prayer has always been a criterion of orthodoxy. The contrary is also true, however, because the development of doctrine updated the official prayers to conform the *lex orandi* to the *lex credendi*.

The present chapter should logically have followed the one on tradition, but it had to placed here because it presupposes some knowledge of the material addressed in the intermediate sections.

Every established religion, be it Muslim, Buddhist, Jewish or Christian, has its traditional prayers, public or private. Each is the product of the faith professed by that confession. Hence any believer may appeal to his particular acts of worship—mirrors of his beliefs—to confirm or deny the orthodoxy of any given statement. To appeal to the formulas of official prayer of the Catholic Church as testimony to its orthodoxy, therefore, seems to be a roundabout argument since the Gnostics, Arians and Nestorians also had their own prayers to mirror their own faith. They, too, had their own traditions and biblical hermeneutics. This leads us back to the initial dispute about parallel or alternative Christianities.

Again, we can take the prayers in the New Testament as models of later liturgies, as we shall certainly do to begin with, but this presupposes an already established canon, to which Gnostics would have objected as they had their own writings excluded by the main Church. Gnostic prayers can be found both in the Nag Hammadi documents[1] and in some of what we call the New Testament Apocrypha.[2] Many of these writings are also attributed to some apostle or other, so we come back to square one. How can we establish a criterion for the interaction between faith and prayer that can attest to orthodoxy? As in the preceding chapters, when we appeal to the books of the New Testament we do so because they are the oldest documents we possess and are chronologically closest to the 'Apostles'.

Of course, Scripture and tradition would be the obvious arbiters, but Scripture, as we shall see in the next chapter, suffered from interpretative manipulation. As to tradition, it was meant to lead back to apostolicity. The fact that both the canonical writers, and many of what came later to be considered as the apocrypha, bore titles with names of apostles, means that it is imperative to ask what apostolicity actually means. It is not merely a chronological feature. It is a theologoumenon. There is a great time gap between the Didache and the Gregorian *ordo missae,* but there is a continuity of principle and an organic evolution. The apostles would not have explicitly thought of Mary as the Mother of God, but had some of them been at Ephesus they would have given their unconditional consent to the teaching. Tradition suffered disruptions when some doctrine or other was considered 'new' or 'recent', not a product of evolution or explanation but as something out of tune with what had been believed or practised from time immemorial. It hurt the sixth sense of the faithful, whether they were simple believers or bishops, who were mainstream Christians.[3] The change of a formula in traditional prayer would catch the ear of sensitive folk and provoke protests. The introduction of Cranmer's Book of Common Prayer in England produced both tacit consent as well as martyrs.

We shall now provide some examples, beginning with the Bible itself. Israel's *Shema'* is a confession of faith and defines Jewish identity. The same may be said of many of the psalms that relate the whole history of the Jewish people from the Exodus onwards. Their faith in Yahweh comes to life in the psalms of praise, thanksgiving and supplication. It is these prayers that separate them from other peoples. Moreover, these same Old Testament prayers were taken up by Christians whose faith dovetailed with that of Israel and formed part of their own confession.

In the New Testament, as well, some confessions of faith were expressed in the form of hymns. The classic examples are Phil 2:5–11; Col 1:15–20; Heb 1:2–4; John 1:1–18; and the many hymns in Rev.[4] They usually emphasise Christ's pre-existence in terms that describe the nature and saving role of Wisdom in the Old Testament which caused so much discussion between Athanasius and Arius at the beginning of the fourth century. The fact that they are in hymnal form, or rather canticles, makes us think that they arose as songs or recitations in the primitive communities and were probably of charismatic and prophetic origin. If Phil 2 and Col 1 were pre-Pauline, as most scholars argue, then 'High Christology' was almost born with Christianity itself and not at the end of an evolving process. Of course, not all communities professed the same level of faith or expressed their belief in the same way, but cross-fertilisation was bound to arise early through reports by travelling

Christians. The *lex credendi*, therefore, gave rise to the *lex orandi* and vice-versa. The texts in Col, Heb and John referred to above seem to have had the purpose of correcting some error or other, and thus from the earliest times prayer points a finger to orthodoxy.

The hymnal genre was not the only form of prayer we find in the New Testament. Paul's intercessory prayers which introduce many of his epistles surely echo, or are echoed by, similar praises, thanksgivings, and petitions of the various communities.[5]

We said above that the Old and New Testaments dovetailed with one another and that the same can be said of the NT writings and the Fathers. We must point out, however, that we possess only a very small part of second-century Christian literature. We know of at least two hundred titles of works that either we do not possess or we have only in translation. Again, we can say that among our extant early patristic literature few books reach the depth of theological thought we find in Paul and John. That had been the time of revelation; now the believers, including the clergy, thrive on sayings of Jesus and flashes from apostolic preaching. It would take time to reach a full understanding of Paul, if that was ever, in fact, achieved. Nevertheless, from what remains of popular or official early prayers, we can confirm the truth of the law of interaction between prayer and belief. The arguments in favour of the *homoousios* in Nicaea, the divinity of the Holy Spirit in Constantinople, the divine motherhood of Mary at Ephesus, Christ's two natures in one person at Chalcedon, as well as the condemnation of Pelagius in later councils, were not based on Scripture and tradition alone. The early liturgy and ways of praying were called upon to buttress dogma.

Maxwell Johnson's book *Praying and Believing in Early Christianity*[6] illustrates these points with appropriate clarity, besides discussing recent literature on the subject. The reader can also find a complete collection of ancient prayers in Enzo Lodi's *Enchiridion euchologicum fontium liturgicorum*.[7]

It is evident that we must first of all point to the above-mentioned hymns in the New Testament, especially the Logos hymn in John 1:1–18, and even more to the hymns in Rev where God and the Lamb are praised together in one breath: 'To him who sits upon the throne and to the Lamb be blessing and honour and glory and might forever and ever' (5:13, see also 7:10; 12:10).

Could the Fathers at Nicaea have been appealing to early prayers when they affirmed that Christ, the Logos and God's Son was consubstantial with the Father? Johnson's answer is in the affirmative. He joins Harry Hurtado in rejecting an evolutionary process of the 'divinisation of Jesus'. Faith in his divinity flowered from the very beginning and was expressed in many ways:

> (1) hymns about Jesus sung as part of early Christian worship; (2) prayer to God 'through' Jesus and 'in Jesus' name' and even direct prayer to Jesus himself, including particularly the invocation of Jesus in the corporative worship setting; (3) 'calling upon the name of Jesus', particularly in Christian baptism and in healing and exorcism; (4) the Christian common meal enacted as a sacred meal where the risen Jesus presides as 'Lord' of the gathered community; (5) the practice of regularly 'confessing' Jesus in the context of Christian worship: and (6) Christian prophecy as oracles of the risen Jesus, and the Holy Spirit of prophecy understood as also the Spirit of Jesus.[8]

To this we should add the invocation of the Logos in the Eucharistic epiclesis. Johnson adds the Latin *Gloria in excelsis* and the *Te Deum* in which praise is first given to the Father then to the Son. These may have belonged to a preface and communion rites in fourth-century Africa.

The Nicene Fathers did not mention explicitly any of these prayers to define the *homoousios*, but the custom of addressing God and Christ together in prayer in Syria, Greece and the West had such deep roots in their minds that the definition only made explicit what the Church, in public or in private, had always prayed.

This was not the case at Constantinople in 381. There the definition of the divinity of the Holy Spirit was principally based on the *lex orandi*, as a result in particular of the writings of St. Basil. Christ's command to baptise in the name of the Father, the Son and the Holy Spirit in Matthew was the basis of all subsequent development of the liturgy in baptism, confirmation and the epiclesis. In Trinitarian theology the variety of meanings given to *physis, hypostasis* and *prosopon* did not help matters.

The doctrine on the Spirit was also refined in opposition to the Arians. If the Logos was created, then this must have been even more the case with the Holy Spirit. The pre-Nicene subordinationist mentality even among the orthodox Fathers was only clarified at Nicaea.[9] In my opinion, however, the query that lingered in the minds of the second-century Fathers concerned more the person of the Holy Spirit than his divinity. The Spirit is mentioned often in the Old Testament. There it means the immanent operative presence of God in the world and in history. In the New Testament the meaning seems to be the same in many passages, especially in Acts. But in the Matthean baptismal formula (28:19), if the Father and the Son are persons then the Holy Spirit should be as well. In 1Cor 2:10–11 Paul comes very close to designating the personality of God's Spirit. Moreover, John refers to the Spirit (*pneuma*, neuter) as *ekeinos* (masculine) in John 15:26.

Some authors, like Hermas,[10] seem to confuse the Son and
the Spirit. Lactantius later developed the so-called 'Spirit
Christology' in which Christ's divinity or pre-existence
was expressed as Spirit. This means that the doctrine on
the Holy Spirit was still subject to development. It took
place as a logical consequence of Nicaea: if the Logos was
homoousios with the Father, and Father, Son and Spirit
were invoked on a par in prayer and in the rites of baptism,
the third Person could only be divine as well. Basil probes
into the ancient doxology 'Glory be to the Father, through
the Son through (in) the Holy Spirit' or in the Latin form
'and the Son and the Holy Spirit'. The Holy Spirit could
not but share in divinity with the Father and the Son.

In 431 the Council of Ephesus shifted from the Trinitarian *homoousios* to the Christological *theotokos*. Nestorius had insisted on two distinct *prosopa* in Christ: one
human and the other divine. Therefore, Mary can be called
the Mother of Jesus but not the Mother of God. How could
the Blessed Virgin generate He who created her? The issue
became a matter of general discussion not only among
theologians but also among common people. It was
urgently necessary to come to some sort of clarification.
Christ, whom Mary brought into the world, was one unity,
and this unity is God and man. As such, she brought God
into this world and in this sense she could be called the
Mother of God.

How did the Council Fathers defend this assertion?
Apart from the logic of the argument itself, the traditional
use of *theotokos* in theological documents and in prayer
was the main contribution. We may quote Maxwell
Johnson's summarising conclusion which well describes
what the Council fathers had to hand:

> At least from the first quarter of the fourth century
> on, then, the term *theotokos* rapidly became a

common title for the Virgin Mary that cut across both ecclesial lines as well as the boundaries of what may be called orthodoxy and heresy. While the term itself is hard to document before the third century, a growing mariological interest was certainly fostered by Justin martyr and Irenaeus of Lyons in their theology of Mary as the 'New Eve' as well as by Marian narratives like the mid-second to early third-century *Proto- evangilium of James*. Hence it could not be surprising at all to find this title in some third-century theological discourse. Indeed, the fact that fourth-century patristic authors of such diverse christological positions can equally employ the term does strongly suggest a common, earlier, and shared history of the term.

Some recent scholars on the acceptance of the title *theotokos* at Ephesus affirm that the term itself was one that was both liturgical and devotional in use, without going into much detail as to how this might have been the case. We have seen that there is no undisputed evidence for its appearance in liturgical usage, although it seems that in some places like Egypt the appearance of *theotokos* in eucharistic praying would not have been out of the ordinary. It would have to be seen however, if it was devotional in nature, that is, rooted in popular piety. But in saying this, it must be remembered, as we saw in the previous chapter, that the early Christians did not make the same kinds of distinctions between 'official' and 'popular' religion and piety that modern scholars tend to make. Nor can we say, especially with regard to devotion to Mary and the saints that it was some kind of lower-class form of 'worship' among the uneducated masses. In this context, bishop, theologian and emperor and the members of the faithful shared a common

relationship of devotion, albeit perhaps with different ends or goals in view![11]

It is right to conclude, therefore, that the title *theotokos* given
to Mary was both a logical consequence of reflection on the
virginal birth of Jesus and of the early prayers of the faithful.
The next ecumenical council took place in 451 at
Chalcedon. A few decades before Ephesus, however, the
Pelagian controversy occurred, in which Augustine played
the lion's part. The British monk Pelagius thought that the
insistence on the necessity of grace for the observance of
the commandments tended to diminish the freedom of
the will and place the blame for our sins on God. Adam's
sin harmed him alone. It certainly did set a bad example
to his issue, but it had no influence on the freedom of the
will or on the status of humans before God. There is no
need for any internal supernatural assistance to perform
good works—at the most, an external assistance in the
form of exhortation would be useful to help to come to a
decision. Moreover, if Adam's sin set only a bad example
to humanity, Christ's death did not 'redeem' us. It set an
example of martyrdom for the sake of righteousness.[12]

Such a doctrine nullified the whole of Pauline theology,
especially as expressed in Romans and Galatians. It is true
that in the first three centuries the Fathers insisted vigor-
ously on freedom of the will, but this was necessary to
counter the Gnostic determinism of both the spirituals
and the hylics. Indeed, theologians such as Origen
preached the necessity of 'providence' for the performance
of good works,[13] and the Greek Fathers insisted on the
divinisation of man as a consequence of Christ's incarnation and redemptive death.

Augustine countered Pelagius' assertions with all his
vigour. Pelagian theologians like Julian of Eclanum were
hard nuts to crack.[14] Apart from his exegesis of Genesis

and Paul, and his appeal to past and contemporary Fathers, Augustine brought in arguments from the rule of prayer. Why did the Church baptise infants, for example? It is true that infant baptism was not universal in his time: he himself had not been christened as a child. That was due to the custom of delaying baptism until late in life because there was only a once in a lifetime possibility of penitential forgiveness. Anyway, if children were christened this meant that there was something in them that had to be cleansed—the sin inherited from Adam. Moreover, the need for constant prayer so as not to fall into temptation, and participation in the Eucharist, made it clear that free will could not make it on its own without some kind of internal supernatural help to heal and strengthen its weakness. Augustine died one year before Ephesus but the controversy carried on later against the so-called semi-Pelagians.[15] The Council of Ephesus confirmed the con-demnation of Pelagianism by two African councils in 416 and by two Popes, Innocent I and Zosimus, in 418.

The Pelagian crisis worked both ways. Many of the collects in the Roman missal begging for grace to be preserved from sin and to persevere in good works find their *Sitz im Leben* in the anti-Pelagian controversy.

The Council of Chalcedon of 451 condemned Eutyches' thesis that in Christ, in opposition to Nestorius, there was only one nature, which was both human and divine, a kind of undefined mixture. The council established that there were two natures—the divine and the human—in Christ united in one divine *prosopon*—person. The reasons given for this definition were wholly based on tradition. It seems that the *lex orandi* did not contribute much to the council's conclusion.

On the other hand, at the second Council of Nicaea in 787 it was the *lex credendi* that came to the help of the *lex orandi*.[16] The Byzantine emperor Leo III thought that icons, by representing the humanity of Christ, fostered both Nestorianism and Monophysism. The iconoclastic era set in and went on for over a century. In the end the decrees of Nicaea II prevailed: the veneration of icons did not threaten the faith and the Eastern Church went back to its traditional prayers to icons of Christ and the Virgin Mary. Unfortunately, iconoclasm returned during the Reformation both in England and on the Continent. Many statues decapitated by Cromwell's soldiers are still to be found in many churches, bearing witness to this period. It would be profitable if those who claim to accept the first seven ecumenical councils recalled the decisions and theology of the second Council of Nicaea.

Maxwell Johnson ends his study with a chapter on prayer and praxis. To assess the genuineness of the interchange between the *lex orandi* and the *lex credendi*, a *lex agendi* is necessary. He writes:

> From the Hebrew prophets through Augustine of Hippo we have repeatedly seen this kind of concern for the verification of worship in the very lives of the communities who offer it. Whether the prophetic critique of Amos, the words of ritual critique and reform addressed to early Christian meal fellowships by the gospel and other New Testament writers, catechumenal formation, liturgical homilies, or development in the concept of the Eucharist as the sacrifice of Christ and the church, the concern that Christians live according to how they worship and believe is, indeed, a consistent concern through the ages.[17]

The examples of the interchange between prayer and believing adduced in this chapter are certainly sufficient to show that the *lex orandi* is a *locus theologicus* and an early criterion of orthodoxy.

Notes

1. For example, Nag Hammadi Library I,1; NHC VI,7.
2. For example, *The Naasine Psalm; The Christian Sibyllines*.
3. For patristic texts see M. Fiedrowicz, *Teologia dei Padri della Chiesa* (Brescia, 2010), pp. 317–320.
4. See P. Wick, *Die urchristliche Gottesdienste* (Stuttgart, 2002); G. Kennel, *Frühchristliche Hymnen?* (Neukirchen-Vluyn, 1995).
5. C. C. Marcheselli, *La preghiera in San Paolo* (Naples, 1975).
6. M. E. Johnson, *Praying and Believing in Early Christianity* (Collegeville, 2013).
7. E. Lodi, *Enchiridion euchologicum fontium liturgicorum* (Rome, 1979).
8. Johnson, *Praying and Believing in Early Christianity*, p. 29.
9. For a complete overview see A. Grillmeier, *Jesus Christus im Glauben der Kirche* (Freiburg i. Breisgau,1990), third edition, vol. I.
10. Hermas, *The Shepherd*, V,1.
11. Johnson, *Praying and Believing in Early Christianity*, p. 77.
12. See V. Grossi, 'Pelagius' in A. Di Berardino (ed.), *Encyclopedia of the Early Church* (New York, 1992), vol. 2, pp. 665–66.
13. P. Grech, 'Justification by Faith in Origen's Commentary on Romans', in P. Grech, *Il messaggio biblico e la sua interpretazione* (Genoa, 2005), pp. 259–276.
14. Augustine's later works, between 417 and 430, concentrate on his controversy with Pelagius and Julian of Eclanum.
15. The Semi-Pelagians admitted the need of grace to perform good works, but attributed their first act of faith to man's initiative.
16. See Nicaea II, *Definition on Sacred Images* in DS 600–601.
17. Johnson, *Praying and Believing in Early Christianity*, p. 126.

9 THE *SENSUS FIDELIUM*

I N THE FOREGOING chapters we often spoke of the *sensus fidelium* as a criterion of orthodoxy. It is now time to clarify this phrase which can be interpreted in a variety of ways. In its broadest sense—religious or political—the concept denotes the reaction of a simple member of any religion, party or movement with a long characteristic tradition to any new proposal. His sixth sense will immediately perceive whether this novelty is in harmony or in discord with his comprehension of that tradition, or, at least, whether it can be interpreted as a genuine development of it. He may not immediately give a reason for his reaction until a more enlightened colleague spells it out for him.

This experience may take place within a political party, a religion or a corporation. The reaction is quite natural and spontaneous. But how does it apply to the religious context of the early Christian tradition, and why do theologians distinguish it from similar phenomena in other religions and attribute it to the Holy Spirit? We shall try to give a reason for this peculiarity. It should be made clear that in this chapter we are not trying to establish the superiority of Christianity over other religions but, rather, to explain the full meaning of the *sensus fidelium* within the single context of the various streams of thought—which were frequently erroneous—of the early Church, and why it is one of the factors that brought orthodoxy to the surface in a world of conflicting ideas and tentative theological proposals.

Some preliminary clarifications regarding terminology are required: the *sensus fidelium* has the meaning outlined above; the *consensus fidelium* refers to the universal consent of Christian believers on a point of doctrine; and the *sensus fidei*, as I understand it, is deep-seated assent, rooted in the hearts of Christians sincere both in their commitment (*fides qua*) and belief (*fides quae*). The qualification 'sincere' is necessary because a worldly careless Christian tends to be out of touch with that dialogue with God which is the real source of the *sensus fidei*.

'The faithful' comprise the teaching Church as well as ordinary believers. However, we saw in the preceding chapters that it was the steadfastness of the laity that served as a corrective to a large number of bishops after Nicaea.

The doctrine of the critical perception of the faithful as a criterion of Catholicity has firm foundations in the Bible, especially in the Johannine writings, and in the Church Fathers, particularly in Augustine. It remained dormant for a number of centuries, except for some tentative seventeenth century references, but was taken up again by J. A. Möhler in 1832 and later more profoundly by John Henry Newman, whose thesis will be examined later.

The doctrine about the *sensus fidelium* is deeply rooted in many biblical passages which the Fathers extended to apply to their own circumstances. The classic Old Testament text is Jeremiah 31:31–34:

> The days are surely coming, says the Lord, when I will make a new covenant with the house of Israel and the house of Judah. It will not be like the covenant that I made with their ancestors when I took them by the hand to bring them out of the land of Egypt—a covenant that they broke, though I was their husband, says the Lord. But this is the covenant that I will make with the house of Israel after those days, says the Lord: I will put my law within them, and I will write it on their hearts; and I will be their God, and they shall be my people. No

longer shall they teach one another, or say to each
other, 'Know the Lord', for they shall all know me,
from the least of them to the greatest, says the
Lord; for I will forgive their iniquity, and remember
their sin no more.

The parallel text in Ezek 36:27 clarifies Jeremiah by
introducing the Spirit and specifying that there will be a
change of heart, from a heart of stone to a heart of flesh,
docile to God's commands. It is also useful to add Is 54:13:
'All your children shall be taught by the Lord', quoted by
Jesus in the discourse on the bread from heaven (Jn 6:45).

The earliest reference in the New Testament to interior
teaching is by Paul in 1 Thess 4:9. The Thessalonians have
no need for exhortation to love one another because they
are *theodidaktoi*—taught directly by God.

However, it is John who actually applies Jeremiah's and
Ezekiel's texts to his charismatic community. In John
16:12–14, Jesus tells the disciples:

I still have many things to say to you, but you
cannot bear them now. When the Spirit of truth
comes, he will guide you into all the truth; for he
will not speak on his own, but will speak whatever
he hears, and he will declare to you the things that
are to come. He will glorify me, because he will take
what is mine and declare it to you.

This text refers to the community as a whole. It spells out
the very nature and genre of the Gospel of John as a
post-Resurrection hermeneutic of the words and deeds of
Jesus of Nazareth by the Holy Spirit in the actual historical
circumstances in which the community finds itself. The
presence of the Spirit does not limit itself to the Beloved
Disciple and his followers alone, but, rather, it extends to
the future Church, in which the Paraclete, the Spirit of
truth, clarifies the nuclear kerygma in the ever evolving

language of the *ekklesia.* It is the foundation of both the *sensus* and the *consensus fidelium.*

However, the ideal community has never existed, even in the Beloved Disciple's time. John's letters make it clear that animosities had arisen within that charismatic Church, animosities that led to a secession. The reason seems to have been initial Docetic views of Christ. Many remained faithful to the Presbyter but others would have no communion with him at all (3Jn 9–10).

The writer of 1John says to those who remained faithful to him that those who had left his community had not been sincerely committed to it; had they been, they would have remained faithful. They belong to the Antichrist who is to appear at the end. But you, who have persevered, he says, have done so because you are anointed by the Holy One, you possess the *chrisma,* the anointing, that enlightens you to remain in the truth (4:18–28). The anointing probably refers to the initial baptism. But the secessionist had also been baptised. Consequently, the *chrisma* is more akin to the *sensus fidei,* the basis of perseverance in the faith that was from the beginning, and in the bond of charity with the Presbyter who had announced the gospel to them. The faithful must not allow themselves to be 'taught by others' to venture into new doctrines that menace the original gospel.

The early Fathers insisted more often on the *consensus fidelium* than on the *sensus fidei* as an argument against false doctrines. We saw above how Irenaeus invoked the concord in the teaching of the Churches all over the world to establish the rule of faith against the Gnostics. Tertullian sums this up in the famous dictum *'securius judicat orbis terrarum'* ('more secure is the judgement of the whole world').[1] As we saw in the chapter on the development of doctrine, for Vincent of Lerins there can be no doubt that universal agreement is a mark of orthodoxy. Augustine also writes that if a doctrine is held by the universal Church, even if not pronounced by any council, it is sure to be of apostolic origin.[2] Jerome explains that the belief of the faithful does not manifest itself only in their verbal professions but also through their customs, popular devotions and liturgy.[3]

In their commentaries on the above-quoted Johannine texts, the Fathers come nearer the *sensus fidei.* The *chrisma* in 1John is usually interpreted as the Holy Spirit received in baptism. But again it is Augustine who stands out because of his thesis on the 'Interior Teacher', Christ, who illuminates the heart through the Holy Spirit. The Bishop of Hippo often says in his sermons that his words can reach the ears of the faithful, but it is only the Interior Teacher who can speak to the heart. Some people in his audience would walk out remembering the words they heard, but unless the Teacher revealed their sense to them these words would remain sterile.[4]

A few scholastic theologians took up the question, especially Thomas Aquinas, but it was only in the nineteenth century that Möhler started the ball rolling again in his magnum opus *Symbolik.*[5] He refers to Irenaeus' *Adversus haereses* I,3,3 where the author says that even those whom we call barbarians, but believe in Christ, have the faith written in their own heart in such a way that if they hear something heretical they immediately perceive its untruth. He also takes up Eusebius' phrase '*ekklesiastikon phromema*'[6] to which Vincent of Lerins' '*catholicus et ecclesiasticus sensus*' corresponds.[7] This does not mean that Möhler denies the teaching role of the hierarchy: he includes the *sensus fidelium* in that part of tradition that the bishops and teachers of the Church transmit as revealed doctrine. Möhler calls this the subjective side of tradition.

Some decades later Newman took up this question raised by Möhler in his 1859 essay *On Consulting the Faithful in Matters of Doctrine*.[8] His main argument was the reference to Pius IX's consultation of the faith of all members of the Church before defining the dogma on the Immaculate Conception of Mary. This time Newman could not allow himself to state his doctrine in generic terms as he was violently attacked by contemporary Catholic theologians on his use of the word 'consult'. It was objected that the term implied the dependence of the hierarchy on the consent of the faithful. Newman answers that the word 'consult' means confirming a state of fact, not seeking advice, i.e., the Pope defines what is already in the hearts of the faithful as an authentic doctrine. A patient 'consults' the doctor about his health, but the doctor consults the patient about the symptoms that indicate his state of health.

Newman also recalls the multitude of post-Nicaean bishops who persevered in their Arian ideas. The *homoousios*, however, survived in the hearts of the simple faithful.

Within the Roman Catholic Church the Second Vatican Council set its seal on this theological axiom in the document on the Church *Lumen gentium*:

> The holy People of God shares also in Christ's prophetic office: it spreads abroad a living witness to him, especially by a life of faith and love and by offering to God a sacrifice of praise, the fruit of lips praising his name (Heb 13: 15). The whole body of the faithful who have an anointing that comes from the holy one (cf. 1Jn 2: 20 and 27) cannot err in matters of belief. This characteristic is shown in the supernatural appreciation of the faith (*sensus fidei*) of the whole people when, 'from the bishops to the last of the faithful' they manifest a universal consent in matters of faith and morals.[9]

This paragraph in *Lumen gentium* is amply commented on in the 2014 document of the Pontifical Theological Commission, *The Sensus Fidei in the Life of the Church*, with an explanation of the phrase within its biblical and patristic contexts, and then goes on to elucidate the doctrine as applicable to life in the Church today.

The phrase does not denote a majority vote or popular acclaim, but, rather, a deeply rooted convergence of faith infused by the Holy Spirit that unites the hearts of sincere believers to discern what is in agreement—or at least reconcilable—with the *regula fidei* and what gainsays it.

The purpose of the present chapter *has been* to clarify the meaning of the *sensus fidelium* in the contexts in which it was mentioned in the previous chapters and to underline its importance as a contributing factor in the establishment of orthodoxy in the early Church.

Notes

1. Tertullian, *De praescriptione haereticorum*, 21, 28.
2. St Augustine, *De baptismo contra Donatistas*, IV, 24. 31.
3. St Jerome, *Adversus vigilantium*, 5.
4. St Augustine, *Sermones in Johannis epistulam*, 3, 13.
5. J. Möhler, *Symbolik (Mainz, 1832)*, § 38.
6. Eusebius, *Historia ecclesiastica*, I. 5, 27.
7. St Vincent of Lerins, *Commonitorium* 2.
8. Republished in 1961: Coulson edition. Cf. K. Kirk, *The Sensus Fidelium, with Special Reference to the Thought of Blessed John Henry Newman* (Leominster, 2010), ch. 6.
9. Vatican II, *Lumen gentium*, 12.

10 AND THE SCRIPTURES?

ONE MAY RIGHTFULLY ask: why list so many criteria of orthodoxy? Are not the Scriptures the last court of appeal? What about *sola scriptura*? As regards the period we are examining, the answer is a set of other questions: which Scriptures? How is a Scripture to be interpreted? Did the Fathers postulate *sola scriptura*?

It should be remembered first of all that the 'Bible' of the earliest Christians was what we call the Old Testament, usually the LXX, with a still open canon. As to the New Testament, it was still taking shape, as we saw in chapter 4. Moreover, in the second and third centuries there was a host of books, mostly Gnostic, claiming apostolic authority. If asked about his faith a Christian would not have answered 'I believe in what the Bible says' but 'I believe in what Jesus and the Apostles said'.

We saw above that the *depositum fidei* and the *regula fidei* determined which books would belong to the New Testament and how they were to be interpreted. Does this mean that scriptural authority was neglected or merely a secondary measure? Not at all! In the writings of the Apostolic Fathers there are plentiful quotations from, and allusions to, both the OT and the apostolic writings. The expression *gegraptai,* it is written, was a seal of authority beyond appeal. Justin's dialogue with Trypho was conducted on an exegetical basis. As regards the NT, however, a citation from the Gospels or from Paul was not yet authoritative because it was written in the New Testament but because it carried 'the Lord's' or 'the Apostles' warrant.

From what was said above, it should be clear that this uncertainty was caused by the circulation of Gnostic and apocryphal books. It was partly for this reason, as well as because of the fact that Christians gradually regarded the Gospels as 'Scripture', that the Jews were obliged to close their canon in the first half of the second century.[1] As a consequence, before the New Testament canon matured in awareness the expression 'it is written' would not have had the same force as when it was applied to *the* Scriptures, that is, the Old Testament.[2]

The next problem was that of interpretation. When reading any script we must first understand what the author meant to say, that is, the author's intention. If the text is anonymous then we have to understand it in all its breadth and all its possible meanings, which may be even broader than what the author meant to say. The classic example is Caiaphas' sentence in John 11:49 to the effect that it was imperative that one should die for the sake of the whole nation. The High Priest meant this politically, of course, but John sees another higher spiritual meaning in the words themselves. And perhaps even he did not envisage the bottomless depth of the atonement.

We said above that the Bible of the earliest Christians was the Old Testament. But did the Old Testament actually apply to Christians given that Paul had definitely proclaimed that no one would be saved by the observance of the Torah? Yet the Church did not accept the OT in parts—it accepted it as a whole. So how were the legislative texts to be understood? Indeed, were even the Messianic prophecies so clear as to be indisputable? The dialogue between Trypho and Justin was based on the Bible, but it ended in a draw. The Jew stuck to the literal historical meaning of the text while Justin re-read the texts in the light of the most recent saving events in salvation history, a method that had been used in the constant reinterpretation of prophecy during the whole Old Testament period.[3] Yet the Apostolic Fathers, from Clement to Barnabas, give us quite a clear idea of how the Bible spoke to the Christians.

The Greeks themselves re-read Homer and the classics allegorically, demythologising ideas that had fallen into disuse.[4] We shall speak later of Christian allegory but a word must be said here about typology. Persons, places and events that occurred in Israel's history prefigured persons, events and locations in the New Testament: Adam becomes Christ; Eve, Mary; the Exodus prefigures the redemption; Jerusalem is now the heavenly city; sacrifices prophesy the sacrifice of Jesus on the cross; and so on. And Melito's paschal homily is a classic example of typology.

The real problem, however, was the Gnostic hermeneutic. This could vary from hardly recognisable Gnostic traits, as in the *Gospel of Thomas*, to the wildest deconstruction: an inside out and upside down reading of the text, as we have already said. The first commentary on a biblical book was written by a Gnostic—Heracleon—and was on John's Gospel, whereas the *Letter of Ptolemy to Flora* was actually a short treatise on ways of interpreting the Old Testament. It is not possible to generalise about Gnostic exegesis.

In the chapter on Gnosticism we tried to give an account of this complex phenomenon. Gnosticism was a theosophy whose core was the Middle Platonism of the day, which incorporated, to various degrees, biblical, apocryphal Jewish, Christian and magical elements. We can say that the Gnostic *a priori* was often imposed upon the scriptural text in order to conform its meaning, plucking it out of its literary context to insert it into an alien one. For example, if the world was thought of as created by the demiurge and not by the Supreme Being, it followed that the serpent in Genesis not only did not deceive Adam and Eve but actually opened their eyes to the truth about their true being. Hans Jonas was not far off the mark when he considered Gnosticism a mythologised existentialism.[5]

We have already seen how Irenaeus countered this hermeneutic by establishing rational rules for an orthodox Christian reading. A biblical text should be read in its literal sense; it should not be interpreted out of context. This context was firstly its literary context, secondly the context of the whole book, and thirdly the context of the whole Bible, the Old and New Testaments. Above all, it had to be interpreted within the context of the *regual fidei*—the teaching of the apostles transmitted publicly by the bishops. These rules were later taken up by Augustine in his *De doctrina Christiana*.

It can be objected that such a reading also imposed an *a priori*—the rule of faith—upon the text. Even if the word 'imposed' is admissible, it was one thing to impose a philosophical idea alien to the Bible, and another to create a new context that derived historically from the same apostolic source as the text itself.

Irenaeus was followed by Origen who is usually seen as the father of allegorical exegesis.[6] The fact that he had the *Hexapla* copied at his own expense, however, shows that he was concerned first of all with the exact reading and meaning of every verse. The historical sense had to be accepted. For Christians the fact that the Israelites struck camp and moved to another place might be irrelevant and an explanation referring the change of location to the spiritual progress of the soul made more sense to them. Historical events were translated into spiritual and moral values.

Not everybody was happy with Origen's allegorical exegesis, though it can be said that few later writers—although they were not enthusiastic about Origen—failed to dip their pen into his writings. An observation is necessary at this point. When passing judgment on patristic exegesis a distinction must be made between homiletic sermons and theological treatises. Origen's commentaries on Romans and John are rich in both theology and exegesis, and further endowed with deep philosophical insights. In fact, Origen himself, following contemporary anthropology, writes that as man consists of body, soul and spirit, the Christian congregation does as well: there are hylics, the simple people who are content with the mere narrative; psychics, or maturing believers who seek the moral sense of Scripture; and spirituals, for whom allegory, i.e. the spiritual and theological sense, is necessary. We must also remember that the Gnostic world was constantly in Origen's mind.

Origen's allegory sometimes resulted in flights of fantasy and pious meditations. A genius like him could allow himself this luxury, but lesser minds often made a mess of things.

A century after the Alexandrian's death the school of Antioch—Theodore of Mopsuestia, Diodor of Tarsus and John Chrysostom—simply rebelled against Origen. They insisted on the literal sense as being the primary sense of all biblical texts. This was not what we call today the historical-critical method; it meant the plain meaning of words in the mind of the author and in the text itself. A row arose around the serpent in Genesis. Origen had demythologised it saying that it was a symbol of the devil. The Antiochians would not accept that—the serpent was a real reptile who could also speak. Even this school, though, admitted a higher spiritual meaning—the *theoria*. A prophet, for example, foretold something that would happen in the near future as a sign for his generation, but there would also be a later higher fulfilment in Messianic times.

Later interpretation moved between both schools or took from both, but it is also true that all the Fathers admitted a spiritual sense over and above the literal meaning of every verse. As was said above, literal sense means the plain meaning of the text as it stands, not the historical-critical method of today. But not even the latter satisfies all contemporary biblical scholars. They find it too dreary. Hence the rise of multiple hermeneutical methods that try to rise above it.[7]

The purpose of this chapter has not been to give an outline of patristic exegesis. It answers the question posed by the title. With the maturing of both the Old Testament and New Testament canons, the Fathers composed more commentaries on the books of the Bible. Some were pastoral sermons, others were of a more theological nature, but all kept in mind running disputes in the Church and with heretics. Their *Sitz im Leben* was the pulpit, not the *cathedra*. Scripture was certainly used, but not in the sense of *sola scriptura*, it swam in the living tradition of the Church—doctrinal, liturgical, moral and social.

Notes

1. Cf. J. Barton, 'The Significance of a Fixed Canon of the Hebrew Bible', in M. Saebö (ed.), *Hebrew Bible/Old Testament: The History of its Interpretation* (Göttingrn,1996), pp.67–83. And R. T. Beckwith, *The Old Testament Canon of the New Testament Church* (London, 1985).
2. Cf. C. Theobald (ed.), *Le canon des Écritures* (Paris, 1990), in which various authors discuss the historical and theological problems of both Old and New Testament canons.
3. P. Grech, 'Reinterpretazione interprofetica ed escatologia vetero-testamentaria', in P. Grech, *Ermeneutica e teologia biblica* (Rome, 1986), pp. 5–39.

4. See 'Allegory Greek and Latin' in N. G. L. Hammond and H. H.
    Scullard (eds.), *The Oxford Classical Dictionary* (Oxford, 1979),
    pp. 45–47.
5. H. Jonas, *The Gnostic Religion: The Message of the Alien God and
    the Beginnings of Christianity* (Boston, 1963), pp. 320–340.
6. There is a vast literature on this subject, but cf. A. M. Castagno
    (ed.), *Origene. Dizionario: La cultura, il pensiero, le opera* (Rome,
    2000),
7. See Pontifical Biblical Commission, *The Interpretation of the Bible
    in the Church* (Rome, 1993).

11 THE EMERGENCE OF ORTHODOXY

THE WORD 'EMERGENCE' might suggest that Baur was right when he wrote that in most Churches heresy preceded orthodoxy which was imposed later by Rome. But even heresy is a negative term, meaning the denial of a commonly accepted truth. Again, 'emergence' implies a coming to the surface of something that was submerged. Can we make some sense of this riddle from the questions addressed in the preceding chapters?

The immediate followers of Jesus were called Christians because they confessed him a prophet, the Messiah and/or the Son of God. Their experience was expressed in language, first in preaching and confessions of faith, and later written down during the first century. Many of these writings were gradually recognised as 'canonical'. It is not wrong to say that all of them preceded the rise of Gnosticism. These early books, and the broader kerygmatic and cultic material from which they were distilled according to the circumstances that required their expression in writing, constituted the main corpus that became known as the apostolic deposit of faith.

However, each author in the first century expressed his experience in different ways. Paul, John Matthew and others can be said to have different theologies, but the fact that they were later gathered together in one canon means that tradition recognised in them a common core, not contradiction, despite their differences.[1] Moreover, one thing is preaching and another is reception and understanding on the part of the listeners and readers. Each person understood the Christian message according to his or her own culture, education and form of mind. As a consequence, it was inevitable that from the very beginning various interpretations of Christianity arose, some of which overstepped the limits of the apostles' doctrinal deposit, even in their own times, as we saw in the first chapter. More difficulties arose when Gnostic ideas began to creep in.

No one understood the problem better than Irenaeus. Hence his definition of the rule of faith and his insistence on the role of the bishops in proclaiming publicly the traditions they had received from the apostles. There were no doctrines that had to be handed over in secret to the chosen few. The teachings of the Church were public. All those Churches that had an apostolic origin professed the same faith, especially the Roman Church, to which all of them had to refer, because it had received its faith from Peter and Paul. This ecclesial network functioned by mutual trust, hospitality and the exchange of doctrinal development.

We know from Philippians 1:1 and from the Pastoral Epistles that Paul entrusted the Churches he founded to presbyters/bishops and deacons in his absence. By the end of the first century, we learn from the letters of Ignatius that a development of Church government was taking place. The college of presbyters that led the believing communities were now ceding to one bishop, helped by priests and deacons. The change took time. Some charismatic communities, like the Johannine ones, were resistant, but they too ceded in time to the inevitable when factions arose in their midst. Mono-episcopacy was not only a social necessity—it belonged to the doctrinal development mentioned earlier.

It was this solidarity among the Churches that helped them to overcome the Gnostic crisis, notwithstanding the fact that many of their members were infected to various degrees by contact with this parasitic religion.[2]

Moreover, a crisis was bound to arise from theological difficulties inherent in the mystery of Jesus Christ. The profession of faith in one God, Father, Son and Holy Spirit, and in Jesus Christ, Son of God and Son of Man, was, and still is, an enigma that challenged the greatest minds of the first five centuries. Both dynamic and modalist Monarchianism proved to be insufficient explanations of the Trinity. The acceptance of the Old Testament in spite of Paul's negation of the saving power of the Torah and the status of extremist Jewish Christians gave rise to Marcion's wholesale reaction to the Jewish inheritance within the Church. Encratites exaggerated asceticism and Montanists did the same with the charismatic element. There were disagreements about the date of Easter. Problems were caused by those who had ceded to imperial persecutions but wanted to return to the Church, especially in Africa. There were controversies about the validity of heretic baptism. The second and third centuries, therefore, were not at all plain sailing.

The real crisis, however, was the rise of Arianism at the beginning of the fourth century. It almost split the Church in two even after Arius' condemnation at Nicaea. But there was more to come. The Trinitarian controversy gave way to the debate on the person of Christ. Augustine argued against Donatists and Pelagians, and so on and on to the iconoclastic movement. Peter's barque rode out these storms but not without injury. We can place the emergence of orthodoxy after Chalcedon and the second Council of Nicaea. By orthodoxy we now mean the universal acceptance of the main tenets of Christianity as expressed in the creeds by the Catholic Church. It was inevitable that pockets of resistance would remain. Nesto-

rianism, Monophysitism, and Pelagianism still lingered
on, but it can be said that the Church Catholic was united
in its profession of the creeds. This carried on until the
schism between East and West in 1054 and the rise of the
'Orthodox Church', among other reasons because of the
Roman addition of the *'Filioque'* to the creed.

In the preceding chapters we discussed the factors that
contributed to orthodoxy. Proposals like Baur's that limit
the rise of orthodoxy to impositions by Rome and the
banishing role of the canon are too simplistic. The authority of the See of Peter was certainly acknowledged and
appeals to Rome from all quarters were not lacking, but
the battle for the right expression of faith in the first four
centuries was fought in the East. Rome's influence was
mainly exercised in the West. Emperors called councils
and Roman legates were not even always present (e.g. at
Constantinople). Majorities were not a criterion of orthodoxy. Even after Nicaea the majority of bishops remained
Arian or Semi-Arian. The canon arose through public
reading in the liturgy. Scripture was certainly the main
court of appeal, but it was also a source of heresy when
badly interpreted. Scripture could only live within tradition—they were united like the body and the soul. Novelty
in doctrine could be assessed as heretical because it was
in discord with 'what was from the beginning', but if it was
compatible then it contributed to the development of
doctrine. In the last resort, however, truth will out. The
series of criteria listed in the preceding chapters, tightly
knitted together, saved the Church's faith from all the
upheavals of history and human weaknesses. They enabled
Peter's barque to ride out the storm.

Orthodoxy, therefore, emerged with its own buoyancy,
a buoyancy inspired by the Holy Spirit. He is the Church's
memory of 'What was from the beginning'.

Notes

1. P. Lamarche, 'Hypothèses à propos des divergences théologiques dans le Nouveau Testament', in Theobald (ed.), *Le canon des Écritures*, pp. 441–494.
2. Tertullian, *Apology*, 37, 4–8.

FURTHER READING

W. Bauer, *Orthodoxy and Heresy in Earliest Christianity* (Fortress Press, Philadelphia, 1971).

R. Brown, *The Community of the Beloved Disciple* (Chapman, London, 1979).

R. Brown, *The Gospel of John*, Vols. 29 and 29a in Anchor Bible (Doubleday, NY, 1966).

R. Brown, *The Epistles of John, Vol. 30* in Anchor Bible (Doubleday, NY, 1982).

R. Brown, *Priest and Bishop. Biblical Reflections* (Chapman, Dublin, 1970).

W. Bright, *Notes on the First Four Ecumenical Councils* (Clarendon Press, Oxford, 1882).

R. Bultmann, *Primitive Christianity in its Original Setting* (Thames and Hudson, London, 1956).

G. M. Burge , *The Anointed Community. The Holy Spirit in the Johannine Tradition,* (Eerdmans, Grand Rapids, 1987).

P. Carrington, *The Primitive Christian Catechism* (CUP, Cambridge, 1949).

H. Chadwick, *Heresy and Orthodoxy in the Early Church* (Variorum, Aldershot, 1991).

Commissione Teologica Internazionale, *Il sensus fidei nella vita della Chiesa* (EDB, Bologna, 2014).

Y. Congar, 'Les saints Pères, organes privilégiés de la Tradition', *Irénikon* 35 (1962) 479–498.

L. N. Denzey, *Introduction to Gnosticism. Ancient Voices, Christian Worlds* (OUP, Oxford, 2013).

C. H. Dodd, *The Apostolic Preaching and its Developments* (Hodder and Stoughton, London, 1944).

H. R. Drobner, 'Patrologie/Patristik' in *Lexikon für Theologie und Kirche* (third edition) 7 (1998), 1473–1478.

M. J. Edwards, 'Gnostics and Valentinians in the Church Fathers', *Journal of Theological Studies* 40 (1989), 25–40.

M. J. Edwards, 'Neglected Texts in the Study of Gnosticism', *Journal of Theological Studies* 41 (1990a), 26–50.

M. J. Edwards, *Catholicity and Heresy in the Early Church* (Ashgate, Farnham, 2009).

W. R. Farmer and D. N. Farkasfalvy, *The Formation of the New Testament Canon* (Paulist Press, NJ, 1983).

M. Fiedrowocz, *Theologie der Kirchenväter* (Herder, Freiburg i.B., 2007).

G. Filoramo, *L'attesa della fine. Storia della gnosi* (Laterza, Rome-Bari, 1983).

W. H. C. Frend, 'The Gnostic Sects and the Roman Empire', *Journal of Ecclesiastical History* 5 (1954), pp. 25–37.

E. Giles, *Documents Illustrating Papal Authority: A.D. 96–454*, (Hyperion Press, New York, 1979).

P. Grech, 'Il kerigma della comunità giovannea' and 'Le confessioni di fede in Giovanni', in *Il messaggio biblico e la sua interpretazione* (EDB, Bologna, 2005), pp. 333–342; 343–450.

P. Grech, 'The regula fidei as Hermeneutical Principle Yesterday and Today', *Ibid*, pp. 147–162.

P. Grech, 'Tradition and Theology in Apostolic Times' in *A New Catholic Commentary on Holy Scripture* (Nelson, London, 1969), pp. 665–700.

P. Grech, 'L'apologia di Paolo negli Atti degli Apostoli', in *Ermeneutica e teologia biblica* (Borla, Rome, 1986), pp. 397–410.

P. Grech, 'La Gnosi. Un'eresia cristiana?' *Augustinianum* 35 (1995) pp. 587–596.

P. GRECH, 'Agli inizi della teologia cristiana' in Di Berardino–Studer, in *Storia della teologia* I, (Piemme Editrice, Casal Monferrato, 1993), pp. 25–98.

R. C. GREGG and D. E. GROH, *Early Arianism: A View of Salvation* (Fortress Press, Philadelphia, 1981).

A. GRILLMEIER, *Christ in Christian Tradition*, vol. 1 (Mowbray, London, 1975).

A. GRILLMEIER, *Christ in Christian Tradition*, vol. 2.2, (Oxford University Press, Oxford, Mowbray, London, 1995).

P. HAFFNER, *Early Christianity. Theology shaped by Saints* (Gracewing, Leominster, 2016).

S. G. HALL, *Doctrine and Practice in the Early Church* (SPCK, London, 1991).

A. VON HARNACK, *Lehrbuch der Dogmengeschichte*, vol. 1. 5th edition (Wissenschaftliche Buchgesellschaft, Darmstadt, 1964).

M. E. JOHNSON, *Praying and Believing in Early Christianity* (Liturgical Press, Collegeville, 2013).

H. JONAS, *The Gnostic Religion* (Beacon, Boston, 1967).

E. J. HUNT, *Christianity in the Second Century. The Case of Tatian* (London, Routledge, 2003).

J. F. KELLY, *The Ecumenical Councils of the Catholic Church. A History* (Liturgical Press, Collegeville, 2009).

J. N. D. KELLY, *Early Christian Creeds* (SCM Press, London, 1972).

K. L. KING, 'Which Early Christianity?', in S. HARVEY and D. HUNTER (eds.), *The Oxford Handbook to Early Christian Studies* (Oxford University Press, Oxford, 2008), pp. 66–85.

K. KIRK, *The Sensus Fidelium, with Special Reference to the Thought of the Blessed John Henry Newman* (Gracewing, Leominster, 2010).

P. LAMPE, *From Paul to Valentinus* (T. and T. Clark, London, 2003).

J. B. Lightfoot, *The Apostolic Fathers* 5 vols. (Macmillan, London, 1885–1890).

J. M. Leroux, *'Le surgissement d'une orthodoxie au IVe siècle'*, *La Vie Spirituelle.*, Suppl. 118 (1976) 294–309.

M. Levering, *Engaging the Doctrine of Revelation* (Baker Academis, Grand Rapids, 2014).

J. Loessl, *The Early Church. History and Memory* (T. and T. Clark, London, 2010).

C. Markschies, *Kaiserzeitliche Theologie und ihre Institutionen. Prolegomena zu einer Geschichte der antiken christlichen Theologie* (Mohr Siebeck, Tübingen, 2007).

J. F. McCue, 'Orthodoxy and Heresy: Walter Bauer and the Valentinians', *Vigiliae christianae* 33 (1979), pp. 118–130.

A. Meredith, 'Orthodoxy, Heresy and Philosophy in the Later Half of the Fourth Century', *The Heythrop Journal* 16 (1973), pp. 5–21.

A. Meredith, 'Clement d'Alexandrie et Origène', in *Mélanges d'histoire des religions offerts à Henri-Charles Puech / sous le patronage et avec le concours du Collège de France et de la Section des sciences religieuses de l'École pratique des hautes études* (Presses universitaires de France, Paris 1974), pp. 393–403.

A. Meszares, *The Prophetic Church: History and Doctrinal Development in John Henry Newman and Yves Congar* (OUP, Oxford, 2016).

B. Metzger, *The Canon of the New Testament* (OUP, Oxford, 1987).

J. A. Moehler, *Symbolik: Darstellung der dogmatischen Gegensätze* (Florian, Mainz, 1834).

V. Neufeld, *The Earliest Christian Confessions* (Brill, Leiden, 1963).

J. H. Newman, *Essay on the Development of Doctrine* (Longmans, London, 1845).

J. H. NEWMAN, 'On Consulting the Faithful in Matters of Doctrine', editorial to *The Rambler*, 1859.

J. O'GRADY, *Early Christian Heresies* (Barnes and Noble, NY, 1985).

A. ORBE, *La Antropología de San Ireneo* (Editorial Católica, Madrid, 1969).

S. OTTO, 'Wozu patristische Forschung? Dogmatische Anmerkungen zur Methode der Erforschung altkirchlicher Theologie', Review in *Münchener Theologische Zeitschrift* 13 (1962), pp. 122–125.

B. A. PEARSON, *Ancient Gnosticism. Traditions and Literature* (Fortress Press, Minneapolis, 2007).

R. PERROTTE, *Hairéseis* (EDB, Bologna, 2009).

M. RICHARD, 'L'introduction du mot «Hypostase» dans la théologie de l'incarnation', *Mélanges de Science Religieuse* 2 (1945b), pp. 5–32; 245–70.

W. RORDORF and A. SCHNEIDER, *Die Entwicklung des Traditionsbegriffs in der Alten Kirche* (Peter Lang, Bern, 1983).

J. SANDERS, *Schismatics, Dissidents, Deviants* (SCM, London, 1993).

A. SEEBERG, Der Katechismus der Urchristenheit (*Kaiser Verlag, Munich, 1966).*

M. SIMON, 'From Greek Hairesis to Christian Heresy', in R. M. GRANT (ed.), *Early Christian Literature and the Classical Intellectual Tradition,* (Editions Beauchesne, Paris, 1979), pp. 101–116.

M. SIMONETTI, *Studi sull'Arianesimo* (Editrice Studium, Rome, 1965).

A. B. SMITH, *A Dictionary of Gnosticism* (Quest Books, Heaton, 2009)

J. STEVENSON, *Creeds, Councils and Controversies. Documents Illustrating the Councils of the Church AD 337–461* (SPCK, London, 1989).

F. A. SULLIVAN, *From Apostles to Bishops: The Development of the Episcopacy in the Early Church* (The Newman Press, New York, 2001).

C. THEOBALD, *Le canon des Écritures* (Cerf, Paris, 1990).

I. R. TORRANCE, *Christology after Chalcedon* (Canterbury Press, Norwich, 1988).

T. F. TORRANCE, *Divine Meaning. Studies in Patristic Hermeneutics* (T. and T. Clark, Edinburgh, 1995).

H. E. W. TURNEE, *The Pattern of Christian Truth. A Study in the Relations between Orthodoxy and Heresy in the Early Church* (University of Michigan Library, Ann Arbor, 2005).

A. VAN DER HOEK, 'The Catechetical School of Early Christian Alexandria and its Philonic Heritage', *HTR* 90 (1997), pp. 59–87.

D. VITALI, *Sensus fidelium, Una funzione ecclesiale di intelligenza della fede* (Morcelliana, Brescia, 1993).

S. WESSEL, *Cyril of Alexandria and the Nestorian Controversy* (Clarendon Press, Oxford, 2004).

L. H. WESTRA, *The Apostles' Creed. Origins, History and Some Early Commentaries* (Instrumenta Patristica et Medievalia 43, Brepols, Turnhout, 2002).

M. WILES, *The Making of Christian Doctrine. A Study in the Principles of Early Christian Development* (Cambridge University Press, Cambridge, 1967).

R. D. WILLIAMS (ed.), The Making of Orthodoxy (Cambridge University Press, Cambridge, 1989).

R. L. WILKEN, *The First Thousand Years. A Global History of Christianity* (Yale University Press, Yale, 2012).

E. YAMAUCHI, *Pre-Christian Gnosticism. A Survey of the Proposed Evidence* (Tyndale, London, 1973).

J. ZIZIOULAS, 'La continuité avec les origines apostoliques dans la conscience théologique des églises orthodoxes', *Istina* 19 (1974), pp. 65–94.

www.ingramcontent.com/pod-product-compliance
Lightning Source LLC
Chambersburg PA
CBHW031851090426
42741CB00005B/447